Alvar Gonzalez-Palacios

The Art of Mosaics
Selections from the Gilbert Collection

Los Angeles County Museum of Art
28 April–10 July 1977

Library of Congress Catalog Card Number: 77-75331
ISBN: 0-87587-080-5
Published by the
Los Angeles County Museum of Art
5905 Wilshire Boulevard
Los Angeles, California 90036

The Art of Mosaics

Foreword

A little more than a decade ago, Rosalinde and Arthur Gilbert began an adventure in collecting through which they have shared intimately in the aesthetic pleasures of the Medici, the popes, the gentlemen who made the Grand Tour, Napoleon and Josephine, and the Russian czars. Intrigued by a few pieces they had bought at random, the Gilberts decided to form a comprehensive collection of Post-Renaissance mosaics. They soon discovered that as far as historians, museums, private collectors, and even dealers were concerned, this was a phantom art.

Encyclopedias and handbooks generally agreed that mosaic art had come to an end "when Renaissance realism supplanted Byzantine abstraction." No comprehensive history of Post-Renaissance mosaics existed to correct this misconception. Evdokia Efimova's catalog of Western European mosaics in the Hermitage, never translated from Russian, is limited to the works in that collection. Ferdinando Rossi's *Mosaics* treats only the Florentine type.

From these and a miscellany of articles, the Gilberts did receive assurance that from the late sixteenth century on there was a flourishing mosaic production in two major European centers, Florence and Rome, but that their characteristic works were so different in materials, techniques, and style that they could almost be considered as two separate arts. Florentine mosaics were made of semiprecious and precious hard stones, cut into varied sizes and shapes and fitted together so that the colors and patterns of the stones formed the desired image. Their subjects were traditionally flowers, fruit, birds, vases, landscapes, and abstract—usually foliate—patterns. Over the centuries they maintained a rich decorative character, for Florentine artists never lost sight of the two-dimensionality of the finished work, the intrinsic beauty of the materials, and the ingenuity required to find, cut, and join adaptable stones. Roman mosaicists, on the contrary, sought to create works that would, in Vasari's words, "appear at a distance as genuine and beautiful pictures." Their materials, tesserae of colored glass without intrinsic worth placed next to one another, were only a means of achieving pictorial illusionism. In subject and style they mirrored the tastes of the centuries: Baroque saints, Neoclassic ruins of antiquity, romantic Berber lion hunts, and a broad range of animals, flowers, and landscapes. Possibly the different character of Florentine and Roman mosaics can be traced to the roles of the two great workshops. The Florentine Opificio delle Pietre Dure was intended from its inception in 1558 to produce sumptuous decorative objects—tables, cabinets, vases, ornaments, and jewelry—for the grandducal establishments. After 1604 it was assigned the additional task of covering the entire interior of the Medici Burial Chapel at S. Lorenzo with rare marbles and semiprecious stones. The Vatican Mosaic Workshop, established in 1576 for the embellishment of St. Peter's, was noted throughout Europe for its mosaic copies of paintings by the great Renaissance and Baroque artists for the altars of the Vatican Basilica.

It was the tourists who extended the taste for mosaics beyond palace and church. By 1644 when John Evelyn visited Florence the Opificio was already a tourist attraction. Evelyn himself set the example for English visitors of his own and the following century by buying pietre dure plaques of birds and flowers, quite like those in the Gilbert collection, to incorporate into a chest in England. From the middle of the eighteenth century the demand for Roman mosaics far outstripped that for the more expensive Florentine pietre dure and through the nineteenth century the independent workshops in Rome flourished. This popularity is to a great extent attributable to the development of the micromosaic. In the late eighteenth and early nineteenth centuries mosaicists at the Vatican Workshop perfected a technique for drawing mosaic glass into multi-colored strips (smalti filati) which could be cut into tiny regular or irregular particles with a sequence of 20,000 tints. With them mosaicists were able not only to attain a higher degree of illusionism in larger mosaics but to create a wide range of small pictorial mosaics to be incorporated into boxes, plaques, and jewelry for tourists and for export to the North.

Having acquired with some difficulty a knowledge of Post-Renaissance mosaics, the Gilberts found that they could see the actual mosaics only by traveling widely in Europe. Leningrad was most important since the Hermitage has the only relatively comprehensive collection in the world. Based on the acquisitions of Alexander I and Nicholas I for the Winter

Palace, supplemented by additions from aristocratic collections after the Revolution, it is especially rich in creations of the most renowned Roman mosaicists of the first half of the nineteenth century: Raffaelli, Aguatti, and Barberi. Florence has extensive collections in the Museo del Opificio delle Pietre Dure, the Palazzo Pitti, and the Archducal Mausoleum at S. Lorenzo. The British Museum, the Louvre, the Prado, the Vatican, the Kunsthistorisches Museum, the Hofburg in Vienna, and other major museums each has a few exemplary pieces. The remainder are scattered in palaces and churches on the Continent and in the castles and great houses of England.

The Gilberts' final discovery was that there was no organized mosaic market. Large portable mosaics were never made in great numbers because of the rarity of the materials and the years of labor required. Of those made, most are either still *in situ* or, as gifts of the Medici or the popes to the royalty of Europe, are rarely available for purchase. The smaller pieces are handled by dealers in gold, silver, and jewelry. They can usually be found only by alert probing in unexpected places.

Despite these obstacles the Gilberts were able to ferret out and acquire a collection of Post-Renaissance mosaics, rivaled only by that of the Hermitage in its historical comprehensiveness, studded with works of the greatest masters of the epoch: Gio Battista Foggini, who brought Medician Baroque to full fruition in creations like the sculptured pietre dure of the Gilbert clock; Nicola de Vecchis and Giacomo Raffaelli, who in the griffin vases and Napoleonic clock epitomize the refinement of the Neoclassic translation of the antique; Antonio Aguatti, who along with Raffaelli is credited with the technical innovations that initiated the micromosaic industry; Michelangelo Barberi, Benedetto Boschetti, Domenico and Luigi Moglia, and F. Della Valle, whose works were exhibited at the Crystal Palace in 1851. These are the leaders, but it is the lesser known and anonymous mosaicists whose quality of design and craftsmanship perpetuated the art. They will all be discussed in the ensuing catalog entries.

This initial catalog of the collection has become a reality through the collaboration of a number of people to whom I should like to extend individual appreciation: to Alvar Gonzalez-Palacios for sharing his extensive knowledge of mosaics and other decorative arts, which has enabled him to date and in many cases to provide new attributions for the mosaics and their supports; to Esther de Vecsey for her extensive rhetorical reorganization of the manuscript; to Alla T. Hall for verifying and augmenting the bibliographic references and footnotes; to Jeanne D'Andrea for preparing the glossary; to George Barkin and Nancy Grubb for grammatical and stylistic editing; to William Ezelle Jones for furnishing the dimensions and marks and for his many hours of consultation with the Gilberts during the period of the conception of the catalog and exhibition; and to the Gilberts themselves for providing the fundamental information they have assembled during their years of collecting. We are well aware of the limitations of the present catalog, which have resulted from the short time available for its preparation. It is being published in the hope that it will stimulate research and interpretation of Post-Renaissance mosaics and thereby become the basis for a definitive edition a few years hence.

I should like to take this opportunity to express to Rosalinde and Arthur Gilbert my admiration for their faith in the importance of Post-Renaissance mosaics as an art form and my gratitude for their generosity in making their collection available to scholars and public for enjoyment and understanding of the place mosaics of this period hold in the history of craftsmanship and taste.

Kenneth Donahue

Acknowledgments

During my research on mosaics and pietre dure, still in progress, I have been helped by many museum officials, scholars, art dealers, and friends. It is impossible to thank them all here, but I would like to mention at least the names of Daniel Alcouffe, Fabrizio Apolloni, Kirsten Aschengreen Piacenti, Luisa Bandera, Giuliano Briganti, Raffaello Causa, Marco Chiarini, the late Anthony M. Clark, Enzo Costantini, Franco Di Castro, Jean Feray, Manuel Gonzalez, Mina Gregori, John Hardy, Detles Heikamp, Jennifer Montagu, Daniel Meyer, Michele Nocita, Marina Picone Causa, Mario Praz, Olga Raggio, Baronne Lilian de Rothschild, Renato Ruotolo, Jean-Pierre Samoyault, Henri-Jean Schubnel, Nicola Spinoza, Horst Stierhof, Pierre Verlet, Sir Francis Watson, Gillian Wilson, Derrick Worsdale, and Federico Zeri.

Charles Truman and Shirley Bury of the Victoria and Albert Museum helped me with the proper dating of the jewelry and the marks on gold and silver boxes. Thanks are also due to Kenneth Donahue and the staff of the Los Angeles County Museum of Art.

Alvar Gonzalez-Palacios

Glossary

Cement
A ground for mosaics made from a mixture of finely crushed stone, sand, and water to which hydrated lime and coloring matter are often added. Variations for interior mosaics and for smaller portable mosaics have been developed, such as the slower-drying cement or stucco invented by Girolamo Muziano in the sixteenth century in Rome. See also mastic and grout.

Commesso di pietre dure
Literally, a placing together of hard stones. A term synonymous with Florentine mosaic. See also Opificio and pietre dure.

Florentine mosaic
A mosaic technique perfected in Florence at the end of the sixteenth century and still practiced there. It employs marbles and semiprecious stones cut into thin sheets, shaped and then fitted together with almost invisible join lines. Natural markings in the stone are used to achieve effects of chiaroscuro, perspective, and pattern. Often referred to as commesso di pietre dure or pietre dure, the technique originated in the opus sectile of the ancient world. See also Opificio and pietre dure.

5

Grout
A smooth-textured cement sometimes used to fill the crevices between the tesserae of a mosaic, giving it a more even surface and preventing the build up of dust and moisture within the mosaic. Color is often added to the grout.

Intarsia
A form of inlay—of wood, ivory, metal, or stone—in which the cut out ground or base material functions as an essential part of the finished design. Most frequently used in reference to wood inlays made in Italy from about 1400–1600. In pietre dure mosaics intarsia and commesso techniques are often used together. See stone intarsia.

Marquetry
A decorative technique, derived from intarsia, in which both field and pattern elements are applied to a ground plane in a single thickness. See intarsia.

Mastic
A pasty cement made of tar and lime or powdered brick, often used in Florentine mosaics to secure cut marbles and gem stones to the base material, usually a stone slab.

Micromosaic
A mosaic made of minute tesserae that enable the craftsman to execute finely detailed pictures, miniatures, and jewelry. These mosaics were first made in quantity during the eighteenth century. Some micromosaics contain as many as 1,400 tesserae per square inch. See Vatican Workshop and smalti filati.

Mosaic
A decorative object made from pieces of hard substances fitted together or embedded in a matrix that hardens when set. While mosaics exist in endless variety, the materials from which they are made have varied little throughout history. The earliest mosaics were made of terra cotta or stone fragments which in time came to be roughly cubical and were called tesserae; glass tesserae were also known to the ancient world. Gold tesserae came into use for accents during the Early Christian period, although gold backgrounds were almost certainly an Eastern innovation. Micromosaics, with their antecedents in the ancient world, came into wide use with the establishment of the Vatican Workshop. Smalti filati, a later development of the Vatican Workshop, added to the mosaicist's repertory in the second half of the eighteenth century.

Opificio
The Opificio delle Pietre Dure, or the Grand-Ducal Workshop begun in 1580 under Francesco I dei Medici, Grand Duke of Tuscany, in the Casino di San Marco, was officially established by a decree of Ferdinando I dei Medici and moved to the Uffizi. Now in a former monastery in the Via degli Affani, it has been operated by the state since 1796 as a craft training school. The adjoining Museo dell'Opificio contains outstanding historical examples of the art of pietre dure. See Florentine mosaic.

Opus romanum
A type of mosaic developed in ancient Rome for use as floor decoration; composed of small glass tesserae and rare marbles arranged in geometric patterns and decorative bands. Similar in type to "Cosmati" work, named for a style characteristic of a group of marble workers active in Rome in the twelfth and thirteenth centuries. Tiny squares, disks, and triangles are used to decorate a variety of architectural surfaces.

Opus sectile
A type of mosaic, used from ancient times, that is actually a form of marquetry. Colored marbles and stones are cut to shape and fitted together like a jigsaw puzzle into geometric or figural patterns. The historical antecedent of the Florentine mosaic or commesso di pietre dure.

Opus tessellatum	The name given by the ancient Romans to mosaics composed of almost identical, regularly cut, rectangular tesserae (approximately ¾″ square) arranged both geometrically and pictorially.
Opus vermiculatum	The name given by the ancient Romans to mosaics composed of small tesserae cut into shapes that are often not rectangular and set in wormlike (Latin, *vermis*) courses that follow the contours of the design. The historical antecedent of the more recent (Renaissance and post-Rennaissance) Roman mosaic and micromosaic.
Pietre dure	Literally, "hard stones" (stones composed largely of silicates, unlike those with a large percentage of calcium, such as limestone and many marbles, which are comparatively soft). A mosaic of tightly fitted cut marbles and rare and semiprecious stones, including agates, alabaster, amethyst, chalcedony, jade, jasper, lapis lazuli, malachite, obsidian, onyx, porphyry, sardonyx. These stones are crosscut into thin (3–6 mm.) sections called *formelle* with a small saw or a copper wire kept sharp by a moist emery. Often used in Florentine mosaics are the following:

Agate

A fine-grained chalcedony used as a gem stone. Banded in two or more colors, blended in clouds, or with mosslike forms. Agates are formed by the slow deposit of silica into cavities of older rock. Because the layers differ in porosity, agates can be stained to produce more intense colors.

Alabaster

A fine-grained, massive, translucent gypsum that is easily carved; pure white or streaked with reddish brown.

Amethyst

The most prized of semiprecious quartzes, ranging from lavender to purple in color.

Carnelian

A hard, tough chalcedony with a bright reddish color apparently caused by iron oxide.

Chalcedony

A quartz with a microscopic crystalline structure; translucent to transparent with a waxy luster; white, gray, blue, and brown varieties. For varieties differing in color because of impurities, see agate, carnelian, jasper, onyx.

Jade

The common name for jadeite or nephrite. Jadeite, the rarer variety, is a sodium aluminum silicate white or green. Nephrite, more common and less costly, is a calcium magnesium iron silicate, white to dark green in color.

Jasper

A semiprecious gem stone of impure crypto-crystalline quartz. Usually red, but also yellow, green, and gray blue. Ribbon jasper is striped.

Lapis lazuli

A gem stone composed of lazurite mixed with other minerals, usually massive rather than crystalline, found in metamorphosed limestone. In color deep blue, violet, or greenish blue, usually flecked with yellow iron pyrites.

Malachite

A mineral that also serves as a gem; the green basic carbonate of copper usually occurring in masses. Translucent or opaque, it can have a silky, vitreous, adamantine, or dull luster.

Marble

A limestone composed wholly or in large part of calcite or dolomite crystals. The colors—whites, grays, blacks, reds, yellows, greens, browns—are caused by the presence of impurities. Among the Italian marbles used in Florentine mosaics and referred to in this catalog are broccatello, giallo, rosso, and verde antico.

Mother-of-pearl

The iridescent lining of the shells of some mollusks. A chief source is the pearl oyster. Like the pearl, it is composed of alternate layers of calcium carbonate and conchiolin.

Obsidian

A volcanic glass or lava which has cooled too quickly to crystallize; rich in silica and similar to granite; homogeneous in texture with a vitreous luster. Commonly black, it may also be red or brown and cut sections can appear to be green.

Onyx

A fine-grained quartzlike agate except that it is regularly banded, often in a contrasting color. Sardonyx contains carnelian or sard, the latter are chalcedonies differing only in color; sard look deep red by transmitted light and brown red by reflected light while carnelian is a brighter orange red.

Porphyry

An igneous rock composed of large, conspicuous crystals, or phenocrosts, and a matrix in which they are embedded.

Topaz

An aluminum silicate mineral with either hydroxl radicals or fluorine, used as a gem. Colorless or a shade of pale yellow to wine yellow; sometimes pale blue or pale green.

11

12

23. **Box with Seated Dog and Butterfly**
Rome, last quarter 18th century
Roman mosaic, pietre dure

Nicola de Vecchis, attributed
Pair of Vases
Rome 1795–1800
Marbles, Roman mosaic, pietre dure

29. Giacomo Raffaelli
Napoleonic Clock
Rome, 1804
Pietre dure, marbles

16

30. **Matched Set of Jewelry**
Florence, 1800–1810
Pietre dure, marbles

31. Clemente Ciuli
Snuff Box with Head of Bacchus
Rome 1804
Roman mosaic

34. Gioacchino Rinaldi
The Ruins of Paestum
Rome ca. 1806
Roman mosaic

38. Antonio Aguatti, attributed
Center Table with Cupid in a Chariot
Rome, first half 19th century
Roman mosaic

45. **Panoramic View of Rome**
Rome, early 19th century
Roman mosaic

55. **Box with S. Paolo fuori le Mura after the Fire**
    Rome, 1823–1825
    Roman mosaic

58. **Faustinus Discovering Romulus and Remus**
    Rome, ca. 1825
    Roman mosaic

20

74. F. Della Valle
Table with Floral Decoration, Birds and Blutterflies
Leghorn, mid-19th century
Scagliola

2. Filippo Lauri
   Rome, 1623–1694
   Baptism of Christ
   Pietre dure, ebony, silver, oil paint
   17⅜ x 20½ in. (44.2 x 52 cm.)
   Signed, lower center: FL
   Promised Gift (G 139)

   Collection: Alberto di Castro, Rome.

   Exhibitions: LACMA, no. 1; V & A, no. 30.

   Literature: G. Lizzani, *Il mobile romano* (intro. by
   A. Gonzalez-Palacios), Milan, 1970.

Pictures painted on slate, lapis lazuli, or other semiprecious stones are known to have been produced in Italy in the seventeenth century,[1] particularly by Veronese artists.[2] This *Baptism of Christ,* however, is the work of a Roman artist, Filippo Lauri (1623–1694), signed with the initials "F L" in the center foreground. It is painted on an oval amethyst panel set in an octagonal ebony frame embellished with pietre dure and silver. This combination of ebony and pietre dure without floral or figurative decoration is typically Roman. Preferred stones are usually agate and lapis lazuli combined with tortoiseshell, most often separated by metal threads.

Extant examples of this type of mosaic were all made toward the middle of the seventeenth century:[3] the best known are the so-called Cabinet of Sixtus V in Stourhead[4] and two cabinets in the Capitoline museums, Rome.

1. Florence, Palazzo Pitti, *Pittura su pietra,* May–June 1970, Florence: Centro di, 1970.

2. Verona, Palazzo della Gran Guardia, *Cinquant' anni di pittura veronese 1580–1630,* catalog by L. Magagnato, 1974; J. Montagu, "Un dono del Cardinale Francesco Barberini al Re di Spagna," *Arte illustrata,* anno IV, nos. 43–44, September–October 1971, pp. 42–51.

3. Cf. other works in Lizzani, *op. cit.,* pp. 5, 16, 75.

4. The National Trust, *Stourhead, Wiltshire,* Norwich: Jarrold & Sons, 1971, p. 31, repr. in color.

3. Grand-Ducal Workshops
   Cabinet with Birds and Flowers
   Florence, last quarter 17th century
   Pietre dure, ebony, marquetry of exotic woods
   Height of cabinet to top of pediment: 30⅛ in.
   (76.5 cm.)
   Width of cabinet: 45⅝ in. (115.9 cm.)
   Depth of cabinet: 15⅞ in. (40.3 cm.)
   Promised Gift (G 112)

   Collections: Second Earl of Winchelsea, Nottingham, ca. 1700; Burley-on-the-Hill, Oakham, Rutland (Sale, Christie's, London, 25 November 1971, no. 91, repr. p. 27).

   Exhibitions: LACMA, no. 30; V & A, no. 40.

This cabinet with nineteen pietre dure panels of birds and flowers and a support with three drawers and a floral marquetry of exotic woods is typical of the Grand-Ducal Workshop production of the last quarter of the seventeenth century. The stand of ebonized and gilt wood is English, late Regency, and the statuettes on the top of the cabinet are nineteenth century, possible copies of older models. A similar cabinet is in the Palazzo Vecchio, Florence. The latter, however, still has its original turned-leg stand and some other obvious differences from ours: it has lapis lazuli columns instead of brocatello pilasters, carved scroll forms on top instead of the classical pediment, and narrow strips of floral marquetry dividing the pietre dure panels throughout. In spite of such differences in details, the dispostion of the panels in both cabinets is identical: in the center, a large rectangular panel with lunette-shaped one above and a narrow rectangular one below; at each side, eight rectangular panels alternating birds and flowers, using the same cartoon in reverse for the left and right sides.

Since none of the birds or flowers on the panels of the Gilbert cabinet are repeated on the Palazzo Vecchio example it is possible that the two cabinets were made as a matching pair, with subtle differences. In the Museo dell'Opificio, Florence, there are a number of panels that repeat the design of some of the pietre dure panels on our cabinet; some were rather crudely incorporated in a nineteenth-century cabinet, others have remained as fragments. The central panel of our cabinet has its counterparts in both a flat and a bas-relief version in the Opificio. A cabinet made in France, in the Château des Rohan, Strasbourg, utilizes Florentine pietre dure panels that are identical to four panels on the Gilbert cabinet.[1] In the Bayerisches Nationalmuseum, Munich, there is a curiously shaped casket in ebony, with fine ormolu mounts from at least the late 1680s, that incorporates three earlier panels with birds like those on our cabinet. This obviously suggests that the cartoons for the mosaics were either used for some time or that the panels were kept aside until needed. Probably both things happened in an institution that supplied a great international clientele over a long period of time.

The cabinetwork of the Gilbert example can be related to a number of similar pieces by the head cabinetmaker of the Grand-Ducal Workshops, Lionardo van der Vin (or Vinne) (see cat. no. 7). He was responsible for the marquetry, which he often produced himself, and for assembling the various parts of a piece of furniture, which in Florence, as in other European courts, were made by different specialists. In an object like this he would have been responsible for attaching the pietre dure panels and the bronze embellishments to a cabinet that would probably have been designed by someone else, for instance, the grand-ducal guardarobiere, but made under his direct supervision; the wooden floral marquetry was possibly his own work. The general aspect of the cabinet implies a rather early date in van der Vin's career in Florence. It cannot be far removed from his famous chest made in 1667[2] and it is certainly earlier than Foggini's activity as grand-ducal designer, which started in the late 1680s.

1. P. Verlet, *Styles, meubles, décors, du Moyen Age à nos jours,* Paris: Larousse, 1972, p. 150.
2. Gonzalez-Palacios, *Tre lavori,* p. 64.

4. **Cabinet with Flowers, Birds, and St. Catherine**
Italy, 17th century
Pietre dure, marbles, gilt brass
Height of cabinet: 22⅝ in. (57.4 cm.)
Width of cabinet: 35¼ in. (89.6 cm.)
Depth of cabinet: 14 in. (35.6 cm.)
m.77.1.15 (G 11)

Collection: Sale, Sotheby and Co., London, 25 July 1969, p. 43, no. 105, repr. pl. 105.

Exhibitions: LACMA, no. 29; V & A, no. 45.

Literature: Sherman, *Gilbert,* pp. 60–61, repr. in color. pl. XXXII; Hillier, *Connoisseur,* p. 269, repr. in color.

This cabinet is decorated with twenty-four pietre dure and pietre tenere panels. On the front there are twelve panels with birds, two with flowers, and two larger ones with vases of flowers. The central panel, with the image of a fountain, is a door on the back of which is a figure of St. Catherine. The door conceals two additional drawers also faced with flowered panels in pietre dure and pietre tenere. The top and sides of the cabinet have larger panels with flowers, birds, and accouterments of war.

Although of Florentine inspiration, the panels were not made in Florence, and it is difficult to identify their place of origin. They can, however, be compared to some inlaid tables that seem to be Roman: the Farnese table in The Metropolitan Museum,[1] and others, notably in the Palazzo Vecchio, Florence, and in the Palazzo del Quirinale, Rome, that also have military accouterments similar to the ones on the sides of this cabinet, a decorative motif certainly not Florentine.

The cabinet itself is probably of North European construction and, like the panels, was made in the seventeenth century. The stand, considerably regilded, is carved in eighteenth-century style with four legs in the shape of griffins with cloven hoofs.

1. Olga Raggio, "The Farnese Table: A Rediscovered Work by Vignola," *Metropolitan Museum of Art Bulletin,* XVIII, no. 7, March 1960, pp. 213–31.

5. **Cabinet with Birds and Flowers**
Florence, 17th century
Pietre dure, mahagony
Height of cabinet: 28 in. (71.1 cm.)
Width of cabinet: 34³/₁₆ in. (86.8 cm.)
Depth of cabinet: 16-⁹/₁₆ in. (42.1 cm.)
m.77.1.62 (G 110)

Collections: Easton Neston, Northants, England;
Richard Courtney, London.

Exhibitions: LACMA, no. 32; V & A, no. 48.

This Chippendale-style cabinet and its stand were made in the nineteenth century especially to display a large set of rectangular pietre dure panels showing flowers and birds. A larger panel of a vase of flowers appears in the center below a lunette-shaped panel with a bird. The mosaics are seventeenth century, made from cartoons of the same period as those used for cat. no. 3. The cartoon for the bird eating cherries, at the bottom right and left, was also used for two of the mosaics adorning one of the two superb pieces of furniture with Boulle marquetry and pietre dure that belonged to the Duc d'Aumont[1] and are now in Versailles. The quality of the Gilbert panels is good, but not as fine as those of cat. no. 3; they were all made in Florence despite the fact that some pietre tenere have also been used in the mosaics.

32

1. F. de Salverte, *Les ebénistes du XVIIIe siècle,* Paris and Brussels: G. van Oest, 1923, p. 167. These two armoires are by Joseph. They appeared in the sale of the Duc d'Aumont on 12 December 1782, no. 113, and are fully described in the catalog, where it is said that the panels are "a remarquer par le bel assortiment du ton éclatant des cailloux et la finesse du travail" (remarkable for the beautiful selection and brilliant hues of the stones and the fine quality of workmanship); they were then bought by Louis XVI through an agent, Paillet (see Ch. Davillier, *Le cabinet du Duc d'Aumont, et les amateurs de son temps. Avec les prix, les noms des acquéreurs...,* 1870).

6. **Table Top with Parrot**
Italian, late 17th century
Pietre dure, marbles
22⅞ x 46⅜ in. (58.2 x 117.8 cm.)
Promised Gift (G 141)

Literature: Sherman, *Gilbert,* p. 43, repr. in color
pl. XXVII; Hillier, *Connoisseur,* p. 171, repr. fig. no. 6.

The design of this table top consists of a central cartouche with a parrot and four different types of plants spreading to the sides. The effect is very elegant; various stones in different shades of green are used for foliage, and, although the disposition of the branches is perfectly symmetrical, the variety of leaves, flowers, and fruits gives movement to the surface so that it does not become routine.

In spite of the sophisticated design, however, this is not a Florentine product. The execution of the mosaic is not meticulous enough for Florence and the Opificio would not have used such a substantial amount of giallo antico, verde antico, and brocatello as displayed here. There is a similar table in the Hermitage[1] that dates from the seventeenth century and is regarded by E. Efimova as Florentine, but the extensive use of brocatello marble alone excludes its having been made in Florence. The Gilbert table top was most likely made in the Veneto in the late seventeenth century from Florentine prototypes. It can best be compared to the altar frontal of the Church of S. Stefano in Venice, which is signed by the Venetian Giovanni Ferro and dated 1656.

33

1. Efimova, *Mozaika.* pp. 7, 92, pl. 9.

7. **Cabinet with Flowers and a String of Pearls**
Florence, ca. 1700 (central panel), 19th century (cabinet)
Pietre dure, mother-of-pearl, gilt bronze, ebonized wood
Height of cabinet: 38⅝ in. (98.1 cm.)
Width of cabinet: 51½ in. (130.8 cm.)
Depth of cabinet: 18 in. (45.7 cm.)
Promised Gift (G 137a)

Collections: Sir George Lindsay, Holford, England; Petit Musée, Montreal, Canada.

34

The cabinet is a nineteenth-century piece of furniture in which a much earlier Baroque pietre dure panel has been incorporated as a central door. The cabinet is decorated with gilt-bronze appliques that include six grotesque masks of fine quality, four on the front and two on the sides; since their gilding has been altered it is not easy to establish the period in which they were made, but it is possible that they are also Baroque. The rest of the appliques, scrolls, and flowers decorated with stones en cabochon are of lesser quality. The dimensions of the central pietre dure plaque inserted in the door indicate that it was probably the top of a casket. From documentary sources we know that many caskets were made in the Grand-Ducal Workshops during the seventeenth and early eighteenth centuries. Some of them were designed by Giovanni Battista Foggini (1652–1725), as we know from his *Giornale,* which contains drawings for this type of object.[1]

The quality of the central panel is quite remarkable. The border can easily be compared to those on a casket in the possession of Prince Corsini, Florence,[2] which has similar bouquets of flowers tied by a ribbon. Equally remarkable is the inner panel with a string of pearls inlaid with mother-of-pearl. It is also useful to compare this inner panel with the side panel on a casket in the collection of Prince de Beauveu Craon,[3] which has carnations similar to the one here. The motif of the sinuous string of pearls is repeated in a large pietre dure table in the Palazzo Pitti and in another table in the Kunsthistorisches Museum in Vienna.[4] The border of the Gilbert panel has a rather coarse restoration at the upper left; its gilt-bronze appliqués with bearded men are certainly later additions while the brass frames that hold the pietre dure plaques are of the period. This panel and the two caskets mentioned here can all be dated to the end of the seventeenth or the beginning of the eighteenth century and are typical of the style established by Foggini.

1. K. Lankheit, "Il giornale del Foggini," *Rivista d'arte,* vol. XXXIV, 1959, pp. 73–75.

2. Gonzalez-Palacios, *Tre lavori,* p. 64, fig. 9.

3. Sotheby's, Monte Carlo, 24 June 1976, no. 262. According to the catalog, the casket belonged originally to Prince Marc de Beauveu Craon (1679–1754), who was viceroy of Tuscany between 1736 and 1748. The masks on the corner of the casket recall those on a drawing by G. B. Foggini in his *Giornale,* reproduced in Gonzalez-Palacios, *Tre lavori,* p. 59, fig. 3.

4. Reproduced in Rossi, *Mosaics,* pl. 75, pl. 98 in color.

continued

8. Giovanni Battista Foggini
    Florence, 1652–1725
    Clock
    1704
    Pietre dure, ebony, gilt bronze
    Height: 37¼ in. (94.6 cm.)
    Width: 40 in. (101.6 cm.)
    Depth: 8½ in. (21.6 cm.)
    Promised Gift (G 137b)

    Collections: Anna Maria Luisa, Electress Palatine,
    Düsseldorf; Sir George Lindsay, Holford, England;
    Petit Musée, Montreal, Canada.

    Literature: K. Lankheit, *Florentinische Barockplas-
    tik. Die Kunst am Hofe der letzten Medici (1670–
    1743)*, Munich: F. Bruckman, 1962, pp. 321–22,
    nos. 596, 597, and 603. A. Gonzalez-Palacios,
    "Attorno al Foggini," *Antologia di Belle Arti*,
    Vol. 1, March 1977, pp. 57–64.

1. Lankheit, *op. cit.*, pp. 321–22, nos. 596, 597, and 603:
    No. 596 (Archivio di Stato, Florence, Guardaroba 1122,
    C. 4S) 1 marzo 1704. Un Orologio, che va legando
    Lionardo van der Vin in sua Bottega di Ebano e
    Granatiglia, alto once 3 largo once 2—con sue Colonne
    di Agata di Siena, che va facendo Aurelio Vestri, i
    Capitelli di bronzo il Foggini, l'altri Bronzi si vanno
    facendo in Galleria dal Giorgi, con sua Mostra di Bas-
    sorilievo et altri lavori simili, il tutto di Duro commessi
    in fondo di Paragone, fatti da diversi lavoranti della
    Galleria, e tutti i lavori commessi sono nelli Armandi
    dello Scrittoio, con diversi Fregi di Agata di Siena, con
    Nicchia di Alabastro nella quale vi deve esser collocato il
    ritratto del Ser. G. D. Cosimo. . . .

    No. 597 (Archivio di Stato, Florence, Guardaroba
    1122, C. 4D) 1705 Riavuto a' 17 settembre il sudetto
    Orologio, legato con tutte le sue pietre con diversi
    Bronzi fatti in Galleria e dal Foggini. . . . con sua Cus-
    todia [sic!] di Albero, che deve andare in Germania, alla
    Ser ma Principessa Anna. . . .

    No. 603 (Archivio di Stato, Florence, Guardaroba
    1123, C. 10R) 17 Settembre 1705. . . . Orologio legato in
    Ebano con Pietre di Bassorilievo, con ritratto di S.A.R.,
    con diversi Bronzi fatti in Galleria, e dal Foggini, con
    Colonne di Agata di Siena, con mostra di Lapis, e Intag-
    liata dal Tofani, con movimento fatto dal Ignazio
    Oliuolaio [sic!]; con soppanno, e Cifera fatto dalla Guar-
    daroba del Elettor Palatino, il quale deve andare in
    Germania alla Ser. ma Principessa Anna. . . . Detroit
    Institute of Arts, *The Twilight of the Medici*, catalog of
    exhibition, 27 March –2 June, 1974, p. 328.

2. Gonzalez-Palacios, *Tre lavori*, pp. 64–65.

3. A. Gonzalez-Palacios, "Fogginerie," *Arte illustrata*,
    no. 59, 1974, pp. 321–30.

4. These vases, identified by C. Aschengreen Piacenti, still
    unpublished, are in the Museo degli Argenti, Florence.

5. The Elector's Cabinet is reproduced in *Twilight*, Detroit
    Institute of Arts, *op. cit.*, p. 348, no. 195. The lining
    that covers the inside of the drawers is specifically men-
    tioned in the original document published by Lankheit
    Barockplastik, p. 323, doc. 615, 16 November 1709 as
    being in "Ermisin rosso con Gallon d'oro."

6. Gonzalez-Palacios, *Tre lavori*, pp. 59–65, footnotes; also
    Lankheit, *op. cit.*, p. 319, no. 575.

36

The face of this clock is a panel of black paragon marble with relief carvings of floral designs in semiprecious stones—lapis lazuli, carnelian, agate, and jade—embellished with superbly cast and chiseled ormolu mounts. The center panel opens to give access to the clockworks affixed to the back of the panel to disclose a red silk lining with an Electoral beret crowning gold brocaded initials: AMEP, which stand for Anna Maria, Electress Palatine. The face panel is set into an ebony case and flanked by two agate columns with gilt-bronze capitals. On the sides are voluted ormolu supports, terminating with ormolu serpents, that are decorated along their descending curves with clusters of leaves and fruit in ormolu and semiprecious stones.

According to three documents published by Klaus Lankheit,[1] this clock was made in the Grand-Ducal Workshops in Florence between 1704 and 1705 for the daughter of Cosimo III, Anna Maria Luisa de'Medici, Electress Palatine. She was then residing with her husband in Düsseldorf, where the clock was probably sent to her.

The method by which this clock was produced is typical of the operations of the Grand-Ducal Workshops. As stated in the documents, Lionardo van der Vin (or Vinne)[2] in his capacity of official cabinetmaker and marquetry specialist to Cosimo III was responsible for all the cabinetwork, while Giovanni Battista Foggini (1652–1725),[3] first sculptor to the grand duke, made the capitals of the Sienese agate columns. The design of the Gilbert clock and of the other two mentioned below can probably be ascribed to Foggini himself; in his book of drawings, his *Giornale* in the Gabinetto dei Disegni e Stampe in the Uffizi, there are various projects for clocks of this type. The design of the grotesque mask in bas-relief on the face of our clock is also akin to Foggini's art. Other artists contributed their specialized skills: Aurelio Vestri carved the agate columns; a certain Giorgi made the bronze adornments, probably after models by Foggini; Tofani carved the face of the clock; and other unnamed employees made the bas-reliefs in pietre dure on the black paragon ground. The last document even mentions the lining of the clock and the initials, which still exist. On top of the clock there was an alabaster niche with a portrait of the grand duke which has been removed. The movement of the clock itself, which was made by a clock maker called Ignazio, has also been removed and substituted by a German clock signed "Joannes Hittorff a Bonn." Ignazio must be the British Ignatius Hugford, clockmaker to Cosimo III.

Stylistically, the Gilbert clock with its extraordinary combination of ebony, pietre dure, and gilt bronze is the quintessential achievement of the Florentine Baroque, reflecting the somber and grandiose artistic taste of the court of Cosimo III. Serpents like those on the sides were used again on the basalt vases made by Massimiliano Soldani for Grand Prince Ferdinand.[4] Pietre dure bas-reliefs similar to those on the face of the clock were carved in Florence for other pieces of special importance, for example, the masks probably intended for the ciborium of S. Lorenzo, which still exist in the Museo dell'Opificio delle Pietre Dure. Even the red silk lining with its gold thread monogram of Anna Maria, Electress Palatine, crowned by the Electoral beret is identical to the lining of the drawers of the famous Elector's Cabinet, which was also made for the Electress and her husband and sent to Düsseldorf.[5] The Gilbert clock can be compared to the only other clock still intact made in Florence at the same time, now in the Bulgari Collection, Rome.[6] The dial of the Bulgari clock has a similar floral decoration and the numbers of the hours are separated by gilt-bronze fleurs de lys, one of the heraldic signs of the Medici. Both clocks can be compared to a third one in the Residenz, Munich, which is missing its original dial and movement. This last example is certainly a work of the Grand-Ducal Workshops, made by G. B. Foggini and Adamo Suster in 1705; the columns are amethyst and the medallion on top is a portrait in pietre dure of the Electress Anna Maria. It has similar architectural components, such as the projecting supports terminating in volutes and chutes of gilt-bronze leaves and fully modeled pietre dure fruit.

9. **Tabernacle**
Rome, first half 18th century
Pietre dure, gilt bronze
Height: 22 in. (55.8 cm.)
Width: 10¾ in. (27.3 cm.)
Depth: 5½ in. (14 cm.)
Promised Gift (G 140)

Collection: Alberto di Castro, Rome.

The front of the tabernacle is designed as a small Baroque church facade with coupled pilasters on either side of the central doorway carrying a simple architrave that terminates in a curvilinear broken pediment. The entire central section is recessed. Atop the tabernacle is a base for a crucifix. The ensemble is made of chalcedony, agate, and lapis lazuli with gilt-bronze mountings. The use of pietre dure with little or no figurative decoration is typical of mosaics made in Rome during the first half of the eighteenth century. Florentine objects of this type invariably have a decoration that includes birds, fruit, and flowers. The gilt-bronze cherubs applied to the top and sides are also typically late Roman Baroque. Comparable tabernacles are still *in situ* in a number of Roman churches of the period.

10. Grand-Ducal Workshops
Cabinet with Landscapes
Florence, early 18th century
Pietre dure, brocatello, ebonized and gilt wood
Height of cabinet: 48⅛ in. (122.2 cm.)
Width of cabinet: 50¼ in. (127.6 cm.)
Depth of cabinet: 23⅞ in. (60.7 cm.)
Promised Gift (G 30)

Collections: Graham, Baron Ash, Wingfield Castle, Diss, Norfolk (Sale, Christie's, London, 4 October 1967, p. 16, repr. pl. 57); Mallett and Son, London.

Exhibitions: LACMA, no. 31; V & A, no. 46.

Literature: Sherman, *Gilbert*, pp. 56–57, repr. in color pl. XXX; Hillier, *Connoisseur*, p. 270, repr. fig. 1.

The pietre dure panels on the front of the cabinet are of a type produced in the Grand-Ducal Workshops during the late seventeenth and early eighteenth century. They are mainly landscapes, often with rather naive figures or buildings on an alabaster ground and in many instances framed with inserts or borders of verde antico or other types of marble. Perhaps the best-known examples of the genre of mosaic are the panels in the Castle of Rastatt (ca. 1710–30)[1] and the almost identical ones in the Museo dell'Opificio.[2]

Apparently this type of Florentine production appealed to a refined foreign clientele. A cabinet, now in the Victoria and Albert Museum, was designed by Robert Adam in 1771 for the duchess of Manchester especially to support a set of eleven mosaic panels similar to ours; one of the panels is signed and dated 1709 by the renowned mosaicist of the Florentine workshops, Baccio Cappelli.[3] A japanned green commode in the style of Pierre Langlois has five panels of this type.[4] Another commode, dated 1779, and made by the French master cabinetmaker Adam Weisweiler, is also decorated with five panels of this type, the central one having a frame with pietre dure fruit in low relief.[5]

One of the most important cabinets in the Palazzo Pitti in Florence, probably made for Grand Duchess Vittoria della Rovere, has a central niche enhanced by fourteen pietre dure mosaics with flowers, shells, birds, and fruit, while the sides have drawers with sixteen panels similar in technique and style to ours. This indeed seems rather awkward, as this type of panel does not appear to mix very well with the more usual Florentine ones. However, the original plan for the piece of furniture, a drawing by the architect Diacinto Maria Marmi (ca. 1600–59), still in the Uffizi, Florence, shows that the side drawers were originally intended to be decorated only with handles. The panels with landscapes that we see on the Pitti cabinet today are specifically mentioned in a document of 1689 (Archivio di Stato di Firenze, Depositeria 1565, p. 23), which enables us to date all the panels of this type to the period 1685–1730.[6]

The Gilbert ebonized and gilt-wood English cabinet of about 1725–35 is set on a regilt English console table of a slightly earlier date. When the cabinet was auctioned in London in 1967,[7] it was supported by a sumptuous side table with balusters and volute-shaped legs united by scrolls and a garland to a central female mask on a shell. This William Kent–style table, which in a way recalls Italian consoles of the Baroque period, has now been separated from the cabinet.

1. Rossi, *Mosaics*, pls. 78–81, pl. 82 in color. The panels were made in Florence and sent to the Castle of Rastatt near Baden-Baden, which then belonged to the sister of Gian Gastone de'Medici's wife, the Markgräfin Sibilla Augusta.

2. Pampaloni Martelli, *Opificio*, pls. 35, 36. A cabinet in the Frederiksborg Castle, Hilleröd, Denmark, is also decorated with panels of this type: the central one with a centaur is almost identical to that in Rastatt. This cabinet is reproduced in E. von Philippovich, *Kuriositäten, Antiquitäten,* Braunschweig: Klinckhart & Bierman, 1966, p. 87.

3. E. Harris, *The Furniture of Robert Adam*, London: A. Tiranti, 1963, p. 74, no. 41 repr. pl. 41. The cabinet comes from Kimbolton Castle. It is reproduced in A. Gonzalez-Palacios, *Il mobile nei secoli*, vol. VII, 1969, pl. 117. The Baccio Cappelli panel is the only one of this type of Florentine mosaic that is properly dated.

4. P. Thornton and W. Rieder, "Pierre Langlois, Ebéniste," *Connoisseur*, vol. CLXXIX, 1972, p. 107, repr. fig. 5.

5. The Weisweiler commode, in a Paris collection, is signed and, curiously enough, dated 1779. It is a well-known fact that late Baroque pietre dure mosaics of all types appealed to the taste of French connoisseurs during the reign of Louis XVI.

6. C. Aschengreen Piacenti, "Un disegno preparatorio per uno stipo in pietre dure," *Arte illustrata*, no. 48, March 1972, pp. 152–53, repr. p. 153, fig. 1.

7. Christie's, 4 October 1967, bought by Messrs. Mallett. The type of table on which the Gilbert cabinet stood reflects the style of William Kent (1686–1748); see the tables reproduced in R. Edwards, *The Shorter Dictionary of English Furniture, from the Middle Ages to the Late Georgian Period,* London: Country Life, Ltd., 1964, pp. 584–85. The side table at Longford Castle, very Kentian in design, dated by Edwards to 1735, has an ornamental mask on a shell very similar to the one on the original table of our cabinet.

11. **Head of an Apostle**
Rome, first half 18th century
Mosaic, gilt bronze
23³/₁₆ x 19⅛ in. (59.9 x 48.5 cm.)
m.77.1.54 (G 102)

Collection: Christopher Gibbs, London.

Exhibitions: LACMA, no. 3; V & A, no. 23.

40

This oval mosaic showing the head of an apostle, possibly St. Peter, is still in its original gilt-bronze
frame with an applied ribbon. Comparable in style to cat. no. 12, the mosaic may be based on a work
by either Carlo Maratti (1625–1713) or more likely by the young Pompeo Batoni (1708–87), who was
influenced by Maratti's classical style. This representation can be compared with Batoni's *Prometheus*
in the collection of Count Minutoli Tegrini, Lucca, and with his *Holy Family* in that of Count Farneti
Merenda at Forlì, both from the early 1740s.[1] It can also be compared with some of the heads in Batoni's
Fall of Simon the Magician, painted between 1746 and 1753 as the model for a mosaic for St. Peter's,
which was never executed. The painting is today in S. Maria degli Angeli in Rome.

1. Lucca, Palazzo Ducale, *Mostra di Pompeo Batoni,* catalog
by I. Belli Borsali, July–September 1967, pls. 3, 12.

12. **Madonna**

Rome, first half 18th century

Mosaic

24⅞ x 19⅝ in. (63.1 x 49.9 cm.)

m.75.135.11 (G 23)

Collection: Antonacci-Efrati, Rome

Exhibitions: LACMA, no. 2; V & A, no. 6.

Literature: Sherman, *Gilbert,* pp. 20–21, repr. in color pl. IV.

The model for this oval mosaic picture can be associated with the work of Carlo Maratti (1625–1713), who provided the cartoons for the mosaic decoration of the second and third chapels on the left in St. Peter's in Rome, which were executed by the mosaicists J. Conti and Fabio Cristofari.[1] The Gilbert mosaic, however, seems to be slightly later and was perhaps executed during the period of activity of Fabius' son Pietro Palo Cristofari, who directed the Vatican Mosaic Workshop for sixteen years until his death in 1743. This picture was certainly produced in the Vatican Workshop and on the basis of style can be dated to the first half of the eighteenth century.

1. Gerspach, *Mosaïque,* pp. 199–201.

13. **A Pair of Architectural Panels**
Italy, first half 18th century
Marbles
92⅜ x 25⅞ in. (235.2 x 65.7 cm.), each
m.75.135.21a,b (G 62a,b)

Collection: Arturo Ferrante, Rome.

Exhibition: LACMA, no. 47.

42

This pair of architectural panels inlaid with marbles of divers colors is of a type that was made in many places in Italy during the seventeenth and eighteenth centuries. It was particularly favored in the Veneto and in the south of Italy, where the Lombard Cosimo Fanzago (1591–1678) had enormous success with a large workshop active mainly in Naples. The exact origin of the pieces has not been determined; they can, however, be dated to the first half of the eighteenth century.

14. **Table with Silenus, Satyrs, and Nymphs**
South Germany or Austria, first half 18th century
Pietre dure, mother-of-pearl, tortoiseshell, brass
20 x 28 $\frac{15}{16}$ in. (73.5 x 50.8 cm.)
Promised Gift (G 138)

Collections: Edmond de Rothschild and Mrs.
Davidson, London; John Partridge, London.

The table top is lavishly inlaid with Boulle marquetry of gilt brass and mother-of-pearl on a tortoiseshell ground. In the center is an oval medallion with satyrs carrying a drunken Silenus, another satyr with a skin of wine, and two nymphs, one of which is embracing a herm of Pan. The medallion is surrounded by a richly decorated field of scrolls and leaves, which in turn is edged by an equally rich border of scrolls and floral designs, with interspersed swans, embracing putti, and grotesque masks.

On the apron of the table are inserted two plaques showing birds picking fruit in pietre dure on an alabaster ground. The tapering, fluted legs and the shaped stretcher decorated with pietre dure and colored marble insertions appear heavily restored and are probably nineteenth century. The top, however, is a fine representative example of Boulle technique as it was employed in South Germany and Austria during the first half of the eighteenth century.

43

15. Miniature Altar

Rome, ca. 1750–60
White marble, amethyst, silver gilt
Height: 23 in. (58.4 cm.)
Width: 15 in. (38 cm.)
Depth: 10 in. (25.4 cm.)
Promised Gift (G TU89)

Collection: Alberto di Castro, Rome.

44

This miniature altar, executed in white marble with extreme virtuosity, stands on a base with three irregularly shaped steps. The bottom of the mensa has elegant volutes and a central panel that bears a royal crown and intertwined initials. The panel opens to reveal a recess in black marble veneered with tortoiseshell inlaid with silver. The central portion of the altar is composed of fluted white marble pilasters and six amethyst columns, all of which have Corinthian capitals in silver gilt. These support an apselike cupola resting on a plinth decorated with festoons and stars in silver gilt, a motif repeated inside the cupola. Two flying putti and two kneeling angels, modeled in the round in silver gilt, adorn the exterior of the cupola.

The purpose for which this precious object was created is still a mystery. It was probably a royal present made without a designated recipient. It appears to have been produced in Rome, where such rich materials were used throughout the eighteenth century. The angels on top recall Gian Lorenzo Bernini's angels on the altar of the Cappella del S. Sacramento in the Vatican. The crown on the bottom panel, surmounting the initials, appears to be French since it has the Bourbon fleurs-de-lys around it. The initials are difficult to decipher: they seem to be *MJL* which may stand for Marie Josèphe, the wife of Louis XV's son, the Dauphin Louis, who died in 1765. The monogram may also be interpreted as two *Ls* facing each other, the initial of the Dauphin himself.

20. **Arch of Janus Quadrifrons**
Rome, late 18th century
Mosaic
19 x 24½ in. (48.2 x 62.2 cm.)
m.77.1.24 (G 33b)

Collection: Amadeo di Castro, Rome.

Exhibitions: LACMA, no. 11; V & A, no. 12.

Literature: Sherman, *Gilbert,* p. 28, repr. in color
pl. X.

21. Johan Christian Neuber, attributed to
    Dresden, 1736–1808
    Notebook, ca. 1800
    Pietre dure, miniatures, gold
    Height: 4⅜ in. (11.8 cm.)
    Width: 3¼ in. (8.2 cm.)
    Depth: ½ in. (1.3 cm.)
    Tax mark: Dutch, used after 1831
    Promised Gift (G 218)

    Collections: Prince Farouk, Cairo (Sale, Sotheby's,
    Cairo, *The Palace Collections of Egypt,* 18 March
    1954, catalog no. 703); Baron de Redé, France.
    (Sale, Sotheby's, Monte Carlo, 25–26 May 1975,
    catalog no. 41).

50

The front and back of the notebook are inlaid with lozenges in varieties of agate surrounding a
central miniature—Marie Antoinette on the front and Louis XVI on the back—in an oval frame. The
spine has a reeded decoration, and the cover has interlocking loops that are fastened with a removable
gold pencil. The pietre dure and gold decoration are typical of the School of Dresden initiated by
Heinrich Dattel (active 1739–69) and perfected by the famous Johan Christian Neuber (1736–1808) to
whose particular style this type of mosaic ("Zellenmosaik") seems very close. The miniatures have been
attributed to Louis-Marie Sicardi (1746–1825) but they have very little in common with the portrait of
Louis XVI, signed by Sicardi, in the Wallace Collection.[1] The only mark on the gold parts of the
notebook is a Dutch tax mark used after 1831.

1. W. P. Gibson, *Wallace Collection Catalogues, Miniatures
   and Illuminations,* London: Wallace Collection, 1935, pl.
   30, no. M 298.

22. Johan Christian Neuber
    Dresden, 1736–1808
    Oval Box,
    late 18th century
    Pietre dure, gold, enamel
    Height: 2¾ in. (7 cm.)
    Width: 3½ in. (8.8 cm.)
    Depth of box: 1½ in. (3.8 cm.)
    Maker's mark: NEUBER
    City stamp: DRESDE
    Assay stamp: 20
    Promised Gift (G 233)

    Collection: Rt. Hon. Viscount Bearsted, M.C.

    Literature: R. and M. Norton, *A History of Gold
    Snuff Boxes,* London: S. J. Phillips, 1938, pl. 40.

This oval gold box has a lid composed of an agate plaque surrounding a miniature of a lady in
seventeenth-century costume. The border is decorated with oval roundels and stylized leaves of
polychrome enamel, and the sides have oval encrustations of lapis lazuli. The box has the stamp of Johan
Christian Neuber, active in Dresden in the late eighteenth century (see cat. no. 21). The mark spells
out "Neuber" and "Dresde" in full, a rare, but not unique, way of signing a gold box. This practice was
also followed by such craftsmen as Schindler of Vienna and the silversmith Valadier of Rome.

Richard and Martin Norton stated that the miniature represents the queen of England, Henrietta
Maria;[1] this does not seem likely. From her dress, coiffure, and resemblance to Madame de Sevigné, it
can be assumed instead that she was a lady of the court of Louis XIV.

1. Norton, *op. cit.,* pl. 40.

23. Box with a Seated Dog and Butterfly
Rome, last quarter 18th century
Pietre dure, mosaic, gold
Diameter: 3 1/16 in. (7.8 cm.)
Height: 1 5/16 in. (3.4 cm.)
Promised Gift (G 229)

Collection: Sotheby's, Zurich, 7 November 1975, no. 84.

Literature: *Art-Price Annual 1975–1976*, Munich: Kunst u. Technik, vol. XXXI, 1976, repr. p. 178.

A mosaic of a seated dog is mounted on the lid of this round box, a butterfly appears on the base. Both have borders of an alternating pattern of three oval and five small round pieces of pietre dure. Around the sides are oval and circular panels of lapis lazuli interspersed with green jasper garlands of leaves. The interior is gold lined. The border and sides of this box are carved in a manner ascribed by A. K. Snowman to Christian Gottlieb Stiehl (1708–92), who "nearly always gave a gently curved contour to the stones he used."[1] Stiehl was a contemporary of the famous Neuber and was also active in Dresden. (See cat. nos. 21, 22). Besides the boxes reproduced by Snowman, a box in the Museo degli Argenti, Florence, showing a similar use of pietre dure is signed "C. G. Stiehl, Hoffsteinschneider." The latter box was given by the Elector Frederick August III to General Pasquale de Paoli of Corsica in 1774; it is therefore useful in dating the Gilbert box.[2] The mosaics of the dog and butterfly are Roman and can safely be dated to the last quarter of the eighteenth century. They are close to works produced in the studio of Giacomo Raffaelli. (See cat. nos. 28, 29).

52

1. A. K. Snowman, *Eighteenth Century Gold Boxes of Europe,* London: Faber, 1966, p. 101.

2. C. Aschengreen Piacenti, *Il Museo degli Argenti a Firenze,* Milan, 1968, inv. 890.

24. Nicola de Vecchis, attributed
Rome, late 18th century
Pair of Vases,
1795–1800
Marbles, pietre dure, mosaic
Height: 20¼ in. (51.4 cm.)
Diameter of shoulder: 8⅛ in. (20.7 cm.)
Promised Gift (G 200)

Collections: Empress Josephine, Malmaison;
Jacques Kugel, Paris.

Literature: Grandjean. *Inventaire,* p. 197, no.
1536; A. Gonzalez-Palacios, "Londra: I mosaici
della Collezione Gilbert e i nuovi acquisti del
Victoria & Albert," *Bolaffi arte,* Anno VI, No. 53,
October 1975, p. 19 repr.

This pair of white marble vases is extraordinary in the refinement of shape and decoration. The slender body rises from a small foot; the volute handles elongate the profile beyond the narrow lip to which they are joined. The handles are inlaid with rosso antico marble, the neck with a band of lapis lazuli, below which are festoons of breccia di semesanto marble, malachite, and alabaster. The central frieze of micromosaics depicts two affronted griffins, each with a classical vase. Between the vases stands a candelabrum, with a swag of flowers being carried by a bird above each griffin. This composition is repeated on the reverse except for variation in the position of the griffins. On the sides below each handle is a medallion with a tripod, vase, and patera on a blue ground. These vases, typical of the refinement of the antique fostered by Pius VI (1775–99) and his court, can be dated to the end of the eighteenth century.

We know that such vases were produced in the Vatican Mosaic Workshop from a document dated 1799[1] which states that in 1795 "the skilled mosaicist Nicola de Vecchis" was entrusted "to make in *smalti filati*[2] two vases in Etruscan style, a subject entirely new in the art of mosaic and a work of difficult execution, never yet undertaken by ancient or modern mosaicists." At the time of the Napoleonic occupation of Rome, Nicola de Vecchis was still active in the Vatican Workshop, where he held the post of *classificatore degli smalti.* Extant examples of vases of this type from any period are so rare that it is almost impossible to find prototypes or parallels for their shape or decoration. There is, however, a porphyry mantelpiece in the Louvre (Salle H, no. 250, Antiquités Egyptiennes) that has three mosaic panels very similar to the griffin band on the Gilbert vases; it is probably Roman, but is thus far undocumented. The design of the medallions under the handles of the Gilbert vases is quite similar to that on the small round box no. 32 and to a small mosaic panel in the collection of Professor Mario Praz, Rome, signed "Giacomo Raffaelli feci in Roma 1802."

This rare type of vase must have pleased the French. In the Salon at Malmaison, where she had the Raffaelli clock now in the Gilbert Collection (cat. no. 29) and a mantelpiece by the same master, Empress Josephine also kept a pair of vases that from the description in the inventory made after her death in 1814 seem identical to the Gilbert vases. "Item, two antique shaped vases of white marble with two handles attached to the body joining the collar of the vase. These vases, carried on two porphyry bases, are inlaid with jasper, agate and lapis in the Florentine manner, having towards their centers mosaic pictures representing fantastic subjects imitated from the antique. Appraised at six hundred francs."[3] The only difference is that the Malmaison vases stood on two porphyry bases which, since they were not a part of the vases, could easily have been separated from them. Indeed, a careful observation of the Gilbert vases shows that there is a slight feebleness in their bases, which explains why it was felt that a further support, which would also match the red inlay on the upper handles, was needed.

53

(detail of color plate)

1. L. Hautecoeur, "I mosaicisti sampietrini del settecento,"
L'arte, vol. XIII, 1910, pp. 458ff.

2. See glossary.

3. Grandjean, *Inventaire,* p. 197, no. 1536.

25. Specimen Block

Rome, late 18th–early 19th century

Mosaic, malachite, marble, gilt bronze

Height: 11⅜ in. (28.7 cm.)

Width: 10 in. (25.4 cm.)

Depth: 10 in. (25.4 cm.)

m.75.135.24 (G 69)

Collection: Frederick P. Victoria, New York City

Exhibition: V & A, no. 115.

The rectangular block is veneered with malachite, the lower narrow element with lapis lazuli. The base is of black Belgian marble on a support of gilt bronze. On the sides of the block are four mosaic panels with butterflies perched in trees against a white ground, framed in red marble. On the top are three mosaic roundels with butterflies and one with a bird. All these mosaics are typical of work done in Rome during the late eighteenth and early nineteenth centuries and are comparable to the butterfly inserted in the base of cat. no. 23.

The original purpose of this object remains a mystery. Possibly it was fabricated in Rome simply to make use of a piece of Russian malachite. Malachite was hardly known in Western Europe before the Empire period; some of the first and most famous examples were the large pieces given by Alexander I to Napoleon, later mounted by Jacob and now in the Trianon. It is tempting to suggest that our object is a Russian work, especially since Nicholas I sent some students of the Imperial Academy of Art to Rome in 1846[1] to learn mosaic work under the direction of Michelangelo Barberi and his assistant J. Bonafede. This workshop was transferred to St. Petersburg when Pope Pius IX authorized several masters from the Vatican workshops to accept positions with the Russian government.[2] Vincent and Peter Raffaelli arrived in 1848, J. and L. Bonafede, Cocchi, and Rubicondi in 1851.[3]

But all this appears to be stylistically too late for an object that has a totally neoclassic flavor, although it is not impossible that the panels with the butterflies could have been copied by the Roman-Russian workshop students who, as we know, did copy for their instruction earlier mosaics, such as a St. Nicholas by the seventeenth-century artist Fabio Cristofari.[4] It is, however, safer to assume that this object was made in Rome in the late eighteenth or early nineteenth century as a demonstration piece incorporating Roman neoclassic mosaics with the exotic malachite.

1. Efimova, *Barberi,* p. 380.

2. Gerspach, *Mosaïque,* pp. 216–17.

3. Efimova, *Barberi,* p. 381, fnn. 2, 3.

4. Gerspach, *Mosaïque,* p. 217.

26. **Cupid in a Chariot**
    Amphitrite in a Classical Galley
    Rome, late 18th–early 19th century
    Mosaic
    8½ x 11⅛ in. (21.6 x 28.3 cm.), each
    m.77.1.74 (G 129a)
    m.77.1.75 (G 129b)

    Collection: Sale, Christie's, London, 24 April
    1896, lot 5.

    Exhibition: V & A, nos. 27 and 28.

These two mosaic pictures, set in reddish marble, are framed with oval borders within rectangular ones. According to the labels on the back, they appeared in a sale at Christie's in London on 24 April 1896, as no. 5. The first picture showing Cupid in a chariot drawn by swans[1] may symbolize the element Air, the second, Amphitrite in a galley towed by dolphins may stand for Water. Charles Avery noted that the compositions are derived from the antique;[2] they were, in fact, probably taken from ancient gems, etchings of which were published in the seventeenth and eighteenth centuries. The Gilbert mosaics, which date from the late eighteenth or early nineteenth century, can be compared to two plaquettes in the Hermitage that also derive from antique prototypes.[3]

55

1. Compare with "Carro d'amore tirato da delfini in diaspro rosso," *Gemmae et Sculpturae Antiquae Depictae ab Leonardo Augustino...*, 2nd ed., Franeker: Leonardo Strik, 1694, fig. 209.

2. Avery, V & A, nos. 27 and 28.

3. Efimova, *Mozaika*, pp. 11, 102, pls. 64, 65.

27. **Box with a Basket of Flowers**
  Rome, late 18th–early 19th century
  Mosaic, tortoiseshell, gold
  Height: 2⅛ in. (5.4 cm.)
  Width: 3⅜ in. (8.5 cm.)
  Depth of box: 1 in. (2.5 cm.)
  Hallmark: a boar's head and a 3
  Maker's mark of Jean-Louis Lefebvre (?)
  m.77.1.86 (G 153)

  Collection: Hancocks & Co., London.

  Exhibitions: LACMA, no. 52d; V & A, no. 99.

This oval tortoiseshell box, lined and mounted in gold, has a Roman mosaic of a basket of flowers, a dove, and a butterfly. The box is marked with a boar's head; the number *3,* which has sometimes been ascribed to the year 1793, although the work is evidently of a later date; and a maker's mark, which is possibly that of Jean-Louis Lefebvre, for whom no dates are recorded. The mosaic is related in design to cat. no. 65 but is not of equal quality.

56

28. Giacomo Raffaelli
Rome, 1743–1836
The Doves of Pliny, 1801
Mosaic, gilt, brass
Diameter: 2¾ in. (7 cm.)
Signed on reverse: Giacomo Raffaelli feci in Roma
1801
Promised Gift (G 162)

Collection: Jacques Kugel, Paris.

The composition of this plaque signed on the reverse by Giacomo Raffaelli[1] in 1801 is taken from an ancient Roman mosaic panel in the Capitoline Museum,[2] perhaps the most loved mosaic of antiquity. In his *Natural History,* Pliny the Elder has described this image as being part of a mosaic pavement made by Sosus of Pergamum, as follows: "Among these mosaics is a marvellous dove drinking and casting the shadow of its head on the water. Other doves are pluming their feathers in the sun on the lip of a goblet."[3] The Capitoline mosaic was found by Cardinal Giuseppe Alessandro Furietti (1685–1764) during the archeological excavations he conducted in the Villa Adriana in Tivoli in 1737. The same cardinal had also found the famous marble centaurs the previous year. In his book on mosaics published in 1752,[4] Furietti stated his conviction that his mosaic of doves was the original Sosus described by Pliny and refused to sell the piece during his lifetime. Many of his contemporaries and later experts like the well-known archeologist A. Uggeri (1754–1837)[5] thought quite rightly that it was a copy made for the Emperor Hadrian. The mosaic was nevertheless one of the notable attractions in Rome. The great connoisseur and diarist Charles de Brosses mentioned it during his trip to Rome in 1739,[6] saying that not much was to be seen at the Palazzo de Montecitorio where Furietti resided except the mosaic and the centaurs. At Furietti's death in 1764 the mosaic of the doves and the sculpture of the centaurs were bought by Pope Clement XIII for the recently founded Capitoline Museum where they are still preserved.[7] The mosaic plaque in the Gilbert Collection, cat. no. 52, is a quite literal reproduction of the Capitoline mosaic including the color and the mosaic frame. Raffaelli has eliminated much of the color of the antique original to suit neo-classic taste.

57

1. For Raffaelli see cat. no. 29.

2. G. E. Rizzo, *La pittura ellenistico-romana,* Milan: Fratelli Treves, 1929, pp. 42–43, pl. LXXI.

3. Plinius Secundus, C., *The Elder Pliny's Chapters on the History of Art.* trans. K. Jex-Blake, introd. E. Sellers, Chicago: Argonaut, 1968. pp. 222–25, Appendix, IX.

4. G. A. Furietti, *De Musivis, ad ss. Patrem Benedictum XIV,* Rome: Jo. Mariam Salvioni typographum, 1752.

5. Angelo Uggeri, *Giornate pittoresche degli edifizi antichi di Roma e dei contorni,* Rome, 1804–10.

6. Charles de Brosses, *Lettres familières écrites d'Italie, à quelques amis en 1739 et 1740,* Paris, vol. II, 1858, p. 38.

7. S. Bocconi, *The Capitoline Collections,* Rome, 1930, p. 101, no. 13A.

29. Giacomo Raffaelli
    Rome, 1743–1836
    Napoleonic Clock,
    1804
    Pietre dure, marbles, bronze
    Overall height: 35½ in. (90.2 cm.)
    Width: 20⅛ in. (51.1 cm.)
    Depth: 8⅛ in. (20.7 cm.)
    Signed on back: Giacomo Raffaelli fece anno 1804
    Promised Gift (G 243)

    Collections: Napoleon Bonaparte, Paris: Empress Josephine, Malmaison; Sir Alexander Kleinwort; Cyril Kleinwort; H. Burton Jones; A. Gifford-Scott (Sale, Sotheby's, London, 15 June 1973, catalog, p. 34, no. 33, repr. pl. 33); John Partridge, London, 1976.

    Literature: Bibliothèque Nationale, Paris, Mss. fr. 6586, fol. 152; S. Grandjean, *Inventaire,* p. 197; J. P. Samoyault, "La prétendue pendule du pape à Fontainebleau," *La revue du Louvre,* vol. XXI, no. 2, 1971, pp. 86–87; A. Gonzalez-Palacios, "I mani del Piranesi. I Righetti, Boschi, Boschetti, Raffaelli," *Paragone,* no. 315, May 1976, p. 42, repr. fig. 34b; A. Gonzalez-Palacios, "Il quadro di pietra," *Bolaffi arte,* October 1975, pp. 42–43, 108, repr. p. 43.

This masterpiece of neo-classic design and workmanship, signed and dated by the foremost mosaicist in Rome, Giacomo Raffaelli in 1804, was presented by Pope Pius VII to Napoleon Bonaparte. Made of marbles, agate, jasper, lapis lazuli, amethyst, a stone of great rarity called labrador, and other rare stones, the clock is a subtle allegory appropriate to the recipient of the papal gift: a triumphal arch dedicated to Mars whose statuette is seen in the middle of the arch and whose sacred animals—the cock, the vulture, and a wolf and dog now removed—were originally represented at the top. The ancient Roman trophies in mosaic to the right and left of Mars and the bronze trophy flanked by two Victories that crown the work enhance it as an exquisite piece of political adulation.

Three years earlier, in 1801, Raffaelli had produced a triumphal arch of similar design and dimensions, but without a clock or attic story. The materials, valuable though they are, are not as precious as those used in the piece intended for the Emperor. The earlier triumphal arch was acquired by the Hermitage in 1936 from a Russian private collector.[1]

The clock exemplifies not only great virtuosity in the carving of precious stones and in the design and fabrication of mosaics, but also in bronze casting: the statuette of Mars, the panoply, the two Victories and two animals all show bronze casting in Rome at the end of the eighteenth century at its best. It is very difficult to say who made these bronzes but it is possible that they were cast in Raffaelli's atelier in the Via S. Sebastianello, for he was later responsible for the magnificent bronze statuettes of the table centerpiece made for the official use of the government in Milan in 1804.[2] The timepiece itself is signed by the best clockmaker of the time in Europe, "Bréguet à Paris."

The clock is described in a document in the Bibliothèque Nationale in Paris written by Raffaelli[3] which defines precisely the forms, materials, and iconography. It is also described unmistakably but in less detail in the inventory of Malmaison made after the death of Empress Josephine in 1814.[4]

The history of the Gilbert clock is difficult to establish from the time it left Malmaison until it came into the possession of Sir Alexander Kleinwort. For part of that period it may have been owned by Napoleon's Marshal of the Empire, Jean Baptiste Jules Bernadotte (1764–1844) who became king of Sweden and Norway as Charles XIV (1814–1844) and founder of the present Swedish dynasty.[5]

Giacomo Raffaelli (1743–1836) was probably the most talented mosaicist in Rome during the last quarter of the eighteenth and the beginning of the nineteenth century. According to G. Moroni,[6] he was one of the first, if not the first, to have worked in "mosaico in piccolo," or micromosaic about 1775. This new technique permitted the meticulous virtuosity that pleased the connoisseurs of the neoclassic era so greatly. Raffaelli, certainly regarded as the supreme craftsman in this technique, worked not only for the papacy but also for foreign courts, like that of Stanislaus Poniatowski in Poland. He was invited to Russia by the imperial government but refused, accepting instead an invitation to the Milanese court of Napoleon, where his technical mastery was particularly appreciated. There he produced his masterpiece —the monumental *Centerpiece of the Viceroy,* mentioned above, now in the Villa Carlotta—and some immense enterprises like the mosaic mural copy of Leonardo's *Last Supper,* now in the Minoritenkirche in Vienna. Raffaelli stayed in Milan even after the fall of the Napoleonic Empire (1814) that had called him there, but he eventually returned to Rome. In 1826 he is mentioned as "lodatissimo fra i lodati" ("most praised among the praised")[7] who had made a table top in grisaille showing the shield of Achilles with the head of Medusa in the center. It is interesting to note that this work is compared with two other masterpieces of the same period, the so-called Shield of Achilles table given by Leo XII to the king of France, today in the Trianon, and the table with the Triumph of Love by Barberi, today in the Hermitage (see the Boschetti copy, cat. no. 66).

1. Efimova, *Mozaika,* fig. 52.

2. A. Ottino della Chiesa, *L'età neoclassica in Lombardia,* Como: C. Nani, 1959, p. 159; A. Ottino della Chiesa, *Villa Carlotta,* Tremezzo: Ente Villa Carlotta [1962].

3. Bibliothèque Nationale, Paris, Mss. fr. 6586, fol. 152, published in Samoyault, pp. 86–88; and A. Gonzalez-Palacios, *op. cit.,* p. 43.

4. Grandjean, *Inventaire,* p. 197.

5. The Sotheby's 15 June 1973 catalog states that the clock was given by the city of Rome to Napoleon on his entry into that city, but Napoleon never visited Rome. This publication further states that the clock was then given by Napoleon to Marshal Bernadotte, but that is impossible since according to the 1814 inventory the clock was in Malmaison after the fall of the Empire. Bernadotte may, however, have received it later from another source.

6. Moroni, *Dizionario,* vol. XLVII, 1847, p. 78.

7. *Memorite romane di antichità e di belle arti,* Rome, 1826, vol. III, p. 452.

30. **Matched Set of Jewelry**
Florence, 1800–10
Pietre dure, gold
Comb length: 4⅜ in. (11.7 cm.)
Diadem length: 5¾ in. (14.6 cm.)
Necklace length: 17³/₅ in. (44.2 cm.)
Earrings length: 2⅛ in. (5.2 cm.)
Marks on clasps and earrings: ET, on a rectangle
Marks on comb: a swan in an oval
Promised Gift (G 186)

Collections: Caroline Murat, queen of Naples;
Delessero family; Jacques Kugel, Paris.

60

All the pieces of this matched jewelry set are of pietre dure mounted in gold. The comb has the French import mark of a swan that was applied after 1893 to objects coming from countries without customs. The clasp and earrings have another mark, still unidentified, with the initials *ET* on a rectangle. The twenty-four panels in pietre dure, some round and some elliptical, represent shells and pearls on a lapis lazuli ground. All the panels are backed in agate, an indication of particular care and quality. The workmanship of the gold mounts is refined, in two tonalities and with a decor of stylized leaves or feathers. The set still has its original moroccan red leather box, decorated with an embossed gold border of sphinxes and amphorae and in the center with the initial *C* and a royal crown. The tradition that this set belonged to Caroline Murat, sister of Napoleon and queen of Naples after 1808, is upheld by a document dated 30 May 1894, which mentions the set and its provenance.[1] Furthermore, the style of the jewelry conforms to the period in question, and the box and its engraved decoration are perfectly genuine. It is difficult to determine, without exact documentation, whether this parure was bought directly by Caroline Murat or, as is more likely, was a present from her sister Elisa, who became grand duchess of Tuscany in 1809 and whose interest in the Opificio is well known.

No other jewelry of this type and of this period has been known until now. Shells, however, were used for the decoration of pietre dure panels in the Opificio during the eighteenth century. The best example is a project by Giuseppe Zocchi (1711–1767) for two tables; one in the Hermitage[2] and its pendant in the Louvre. The original cartoons for these two table tops have been recently rediscovered by the writer; they are in the Museo dell'Opificio, always recognized as by the hand of Giuseppe Zocchi. In the Prado there are two table tops that have fine borders with fruits and shells on a lapis lazuli ground.[3] In the archives of the Museo dell'Opificio there are also some drawings[4] that show that this type of shell decoration was projected for boxes, tables and jewelry. One of these drawings has indeed much in common with the central plaques of the Gilbert diadem, comb, and necklace. The drawing is not signed, but it is dated 22 October 1798. It is most likely by Leopoldo Cioci who, in 1792, succeeded his father Antonio as "disegnatore e scegliatore di pietre" (designer and selector of stones) in the Opificio,[5] and who probably designed various table tops in the Palazzo Pitti. The style of this set of jewelry is, in fact, most characteristic of the tradition established by Giuseppe Zocchi and Antonio Cioci and continued by Leopoldo Cioci in the Opificio in the late eighteenth century.

1. Extract of the will of M. Gabriel Delessert of the family of the banker to the emperor, in the archives of the Los Angeles County Museum of Art. It is interesting to note that the will dates from 1894 while the swan mark on some of the jewelry is from the previous year, which means that these objects were probably not kept in France.

2. Efimova, *Mozaika*, pp. 8, 93, pl. 15. The Hermitage table has been enlarged to make it a square. Its pendant in the Louvre, with flowers and butterflies on an alabaster ground, still has its original shape.

3. Rossi, *Mosaics*, pl. 97 in color.

4. A. Martelli Pampaloni, "Tarsie neoclassiche in pietra dura," *Kalòs*, no. 13, June 1972, p. 1.

5. For Leopold Cioci, see Rossi, *Mosaics*, pp. 167–68.

31. Clemente Ciuli
Snuff Box with Head of Bacchus
Rome, 1804
Mosaic, enamel, gold
Diameter: 3¼ in. (8.3 cm.)
Depth of box: ¾ in. (1.9 cm.)
Signed: C. Ciuli Romano F. A. 1804
Maker's mark of Adrien-Jean-Maximilian Vachette
Promised Gift (G 75)

Collections: Pius VII, Rome; Mr. Mussland;
Mr. Garrard, London.

Exhibitions: LACMA, no. 51; V & A, no. 69;
LACMA, *Decade,* catalog no. 82, p. 194, repr. in
color p. 88.

Literature: Hillier, *Connoisseur,* p. 273, repr. in
color.

62

The Roman mosaic lid of this round box is framed in gold and blue enamel, and the base is decorated with a delicate enamel amphora with an elaborate classical ornamental frieze. The box bears the marks of the goldsmith Adrien-Jean-Maximilian Vachette, active between 1779 and 1839. The mosaic depicts the head of Bacchus in profile to the left, crowned with a wreath of vines, grapes, and leaves, all on a dark ground. It is signed "C. Ciuli Romano F. A. 1804." Clemente Ciuli, who had a shop in the Piazza di Spagna, was a very well known mosaicist in the early nineteenth century. G. A. Guattani not only identifies him as one of the mosaicists "in piccolo" then active in Rome, but even describes in detail a head of Jupiter done in monochrome mosaic like our Bacchus. Guattani considered Ciuli the best mosaicist in this particular type of monochrome work and points out that the minuteness, the evenness, and the connection of the tesserae were so perfect that the mosaic seemed like a drawing.[1] Unfortunately, there is only one other work by Clemente Ciuli that can be used for comparison: a small picture of a vestal in the Galerie de Mineralogie of the Jardin des Plantes in Paris; this fine work is signed and dated 1828.

In the inventory of Malmaison taken after Josphine's death in 1814, there is listed a mosaic very much like ours, described as "une mosaïque circulaire en camayeu gris sur fond bleu, encadrée, représentant une tête de Bacchus." (. . . a round mosaic in monochrome grey on blue background, framed, depicting a head of Bacchus.) It would be tempting to attribute it to Ciuli.[2]

According to a letter in French dated 2 July 1811 in the Los Angeles County Museum of Art archives, our box was given by Pius VII to a person whose signature unfortunately is undecipherable; he in turn gave it to a certain Mr. Mussland as a token of gratitude for financial help.

1. Guattani, *Memorie,* vol. IV, pp. 57–157.
2. Grandjean, *Inventaire,* no. 1398, p. 183.

32. Box with the Altar of Love
  Rome, early 19th century
  Mosaic, tortoiseshell, gold
  Diameter: 3 in. (7.6 cm.)
  Depth of box: 1 in. (2.5 cm.)
  m.77.1.57 (G 105b)

  Collection: E. & H. Graus, London.

The Roman mosaic on this tortoiseshell box with a gold lid represents the Altar of Love with Cupid's bow and arrow atop the altar and Venus's doves billing below it. It provided the donor with a vehicle for expressing affection with typical neoclassical restraint. Since the border is identical with that used in Raffaelli's *Doves of Pliny* (cat. no. 28) and the box is contemporary with that master it could have been produced in his shop after his design.

33. François Belloni, attributed
Rome and Paris, 1772–1832
Guéridon
Mosaic, rosewood
Diameter: 24¹/₃₂ in. (61.1 cm.)
Height of table: 28⅜ in. (72.7 cm.)
m.75.135.23 (G 68)

Collections: Dudley Long, Glenham Hall, Suffolk,
England; Mallet and Son, London, England.

Exhibitions: LACMA, no. 36; V & A, no. 36.

Literature: Sherman, *Gilbert,* pp. 48–49, repr. in
color pl. XXIV; Hillier, *Connoisseur,* p. 268, repr.
in color p. 269.

64

On the octagonal mosaic table top Hebe, the cupbearer of the gods, appears in the central medallion, encircled by a border with a fluttering ribbon connecting four insignia: the crown and thunderbolt of Jupiter, king of the gods, and the caduceus and scales of Mercury, messenger of the gods and god of commerce. Four lunettes along the outer border enclose avian attributes of antique gods. Jupiter's eagle, about to drink from Hebe's cup; Apollo's swan; Juno's peacocks; and Venus's doves. The figure of Hebe is modeled after a famous statue by Antonio Canova (1757–1822), of which there are several versions. The oldest of these was made between 1795 and 1799 for Giuseppe Albrizzi; it was in Venice from 1799 to 1830 and is now in the Nationalgalerie in East Berlin.[1] Canova made a second version for Empress Josephine, which was in Paris at Malmaison[2] from 1805 to 1814. It is difficult to state which sculpture by Canova might have served as inspiration for the Gilbert Hebe.

Although the assumption is that the mosaic table is Roman, the style does not correspond to anything produced in Rome. Another possibility points to an Italian mosaicist named Belloni, who was active in France in the early nineteenth century. The model for the Hebe might have been the version in France, and it is possible that the table itself was made there by Belloni. He had apparently worked in the Vatican Workshop and moved to Paris in 1798. There he opened a workshop which had considerable success and was active until 1832. He executed a mosaic pavement, his most famous work, for the Salle de Melpomène in the Louvre,[3] now in storage at Compiegnes, another in front of the Galerie d'Apollon. He was obviously known to the Empress, who owned two table tops by Belloni; one is unidentified, but the other is described in one of the entries of the inventory of Malmaison at the death of Josephine: "A round table in white marble, decorated with five scenes in mosaic and other accessories also done in mosaic, the principal scene representing a dancer copied from a painting in Herculaneum, and the four small ones representing birds; this table, designed and executed by Belloni, is placed on a rosewood pedestal decorated with gilt bronze."[4] Indeed this description is very similar to the table top here, but until further documentary evidence or signed works by Belloni appear a certain attribution of this piece to him cannot be made. The pedestal of rosewood veneer and gilt wood is English and can be dated about 1820. The table comes from Glenham Hall, Suffolk, which belonged to Dudley Long from 1789 to 1829; it was probably during those years that the mosaic came to England and the Regency pedestal was made.

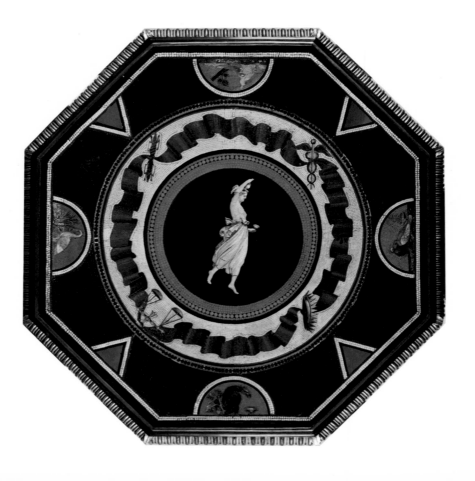

1. M. Praz and G. Pavonello, *L'opera completa del Canova,* Milan: Rizzoli, 1976, no. 98, repr.

2. H. Honour, *The Age of Neoclassicism,* London: The Arts Council of Great Britain, 1972, pp. 204–5, no. 317.

3. E. Gerspach, "Les mosaïques de Belloni," *Gazettes des Beaux Arts,* ser. 2, vol. 37, 1888, pp. 55–59.

4. S. Grandjean, *Inventaire,* p. 193, no. 1501.

34. Gioacchino Rinaldi
Rome, active late 18th–early 19th century
The Ruins of Paestum,
ca. 1805
Mosaic
19⅜ x 64¼ in. (49.2 x 163.2 cm.)
Signed, lower right: G. Rinaldi
Promised Gift (G 199)

Collections: South Audley Art Galleries, London
(Sale, Phillips, London, 25 March 1975, no. 154).

Literature: Guattani, *Memorie,* vol. I, p. 20.

This mosaic picture, which represents the three Greek temples of Paestum and is signed "G. Rinaldi," was fully described by G. A. Guattani, who wrote in 1805 that the mosaic picture was a "caminiera," i.e., it was intended to be hung over a mantelpiece. The composition was taken from a painting by the Russian artist Fedor M. Matveev (1758–1826) commissioned by Count Hervet, the earl of Bristol. Rinaldi had taken five years to complete this work. According to Guattani, it was the best mosaic he had thus far made and in its pictorial effects was superior to Matveev's original.[1] There are four other versions of this picture: one in the possession of John Alsop, Long Island; another at Anglesey Abbey, Cambridge, the home of Lord Fairhaven; a third in Sans Souci; and the fourth in the Hermitage.

E. Efimova dated the Hermitage version to 1830; It was acquired in Italy in 1838 by Prince K. A. Liven. She mentions two replicas, one in Sans Souci, and the other on loan to The Metropolitan Museum of Art, which has since been returned to its owner, John Alsop.[2]

The Gilbert mosaic and the one in the Hermitage are identical; it is therefore impossible to say which is the one made first by Rinaldi and described in 1806 by Guattani. Gioacchino Rinaldi was an artist of considerable success in the early nineteenth century. In 1806 his work, according to Guattani,[3] included other important achievements: another caminiera picture with an eruption of Vesuvius, also after a picture by F. M. Matveev; a view of the Colosseum; another of the Ponte Molle; and a view of the Campo Vecchio with a frame enhanced by an important cameo of Vespasian supported by two sphinxes. Three years later Guattani[4] added that two mantelpieces by Rinaldi were in Paris and that he had been commissioned to translate a portrait of Napoleon by Robert Lefebvre into mosaic, which was completed and ready to be taken to Paris.

The duration of Gioacchino Rinaldi's artistic activity has not yet been determined. A Constantino Rinaldi was mentioned by Moroni in 1847;[5] he was listed in 1867 as having a shop in the Via del Babuino, no. 125, and as being "much employed by the government and public establishments in restoring ancient mosaics."[6] He was probably a son of Gioacchino or a member of the same family, for mosaicists, like many other craftsmen, were often active in the same field for more than one generation.

65

1. Guattani, *Memorie,* vol. I, p. 43.

2. Efimova, *Mozaika,* pp. 11, 102, pl. 67.

3. Guattani, *Memorie,* vol. II, p. 11.

4. *Ibid.,* vol. V, p. 14.

5. Moroni, *Dizionario,* vol. XLVII, p. 80.

6. Murray, *Handbook,* 1867, p. XXVI.

35. Antonio Aguatti
Rome, active first half 19th century
Box with a Poodle and a Spaniel
Mosaic, gold
Diameter: 3³/₃₂ in. (8.1 cm.)
Depth of box: 3⅛ in. (8 cm.)
Signed, lower right: AGUATTI
Promised Gift (G 175)

Collection: James Robinson, New York.

66

This round mosaic plaque shows a spaniel and a poodle in a landscape in the Roman Campagna. The gold mount is modern. The mosaic is signed "Aguatti," the name of a family of mosaicists active in Rome in the eighteenth and nineteenth centuries. Cesare Aguatti was the author of the superb mosaics in the Hall of the Emperors in the Villa Borghese that were commissioned by Prince Marcantonio Borghese during the restoration of that famous palace about 1782.[1] Our plaque is almost certainly by Antonio Aguatti, who is mentioned by G. A. Guattani[2] as a mosaicist "in piccolo," which means that he was a specialist with tiny tesserae in contrast to the Vatican masters who were, according to Guattani, mosaicists "in grande." Antonio Aguatti had a workshop of his own but he seems to have worked also for the Vatican. In 1847 Moroni considered him "the master of today's artisans," especially for his technical innovations. "In the workshop of this worthy artist an improvement was made in the stripped smalti, notable not only because it increased the number of geometric shapes, but also, through combining colors and more half-tones in the same strip [filato], it facilitated the making of flowers, trees, buildings, and especially of furry animals, by imitating the movement of hair with single pieces which have a chiaroscuro obtained from the aforementioned impasto of more than one shade in a single strip."[3] The latter is clearly visible in the Gilbert plaque.

Antonio Aguatti was the master of Michelangelo Barberi (active 1820–60), who succeeded him as the most renowned mosaic artist in Rome and who dedicated a booklet that he published in 1823 to Aguatti with words full of praise and gratitude. In addition to the other mosaic signed by Aguatti in the Gilbert Collection (cat. no. 36), there is also a signed round table top in the Hermitage with Cupid in a chariot guided by tigers.[4]

1. P. della Pergola, *Villa Borghese, Guida Storico–Artistica*, Florence: Sadea, 1966, fig. 22.

2. Guattani, *Memorie*, vol. IV, p. 156.

3. Moroni, *Dizionario*, vol. XLVII, 1847, pp. 78–79.

4. Efimova, *Mozaika*, pp. 10, 99, pl. 48.

36. Antonio Aguatti
   Rome, active first half 19th century
   Box with a Spaniel
   Mosaic, tortoiseshell, gold
   Height: 2³/₁₆ in. (5.6 cm.)
   Width: 2⅞ in. (7.3 cm.)
   Depth of box: 1³/₁₆ in. (3 cm.)
   Signed, lower center: aguatti
   m.77.1.66 (G 123a)

   Exhibition: V & A, no. 88.

This oval tortoiseshell box with unmarked gold mounts displays a Roman mosaic plaque with a spaniel in a landscape, signed "aguatti." This is evidently Antonio Aguatti, who was active in Rome during the first half of the nineteenth century and was noted for his mosaics of animals (see cat. no. 35).

37. Antonio Aguatti, attributed to
Rome, active first half 19th century
Necklace with Landscapes, ca. 1800–10
Mosaic, blue glass, gold
Length: 18⅛ in. (46 cm.)
m.77.1.80 (G 142)

Collection: Hancocks & Co., London.

Exhibitions: LACMA, no. 52a; V & A, no. 60.

Literature: C. Gere, *European and American Jewelry,
1830–1914,* London: Heinemann, 1975, p. 127.

This necklace is composed of nine oval Roman mosaic plaques with landscapes of the Campagna and one of a spaniel on the clasp; all are set in blue glass and mounted in plain gold filets. The mosaic on the clasp is similar to the spaniels depicted in cat. nos. 35 and 36, both of which are signed "Aguatti." The exceptional quality of the plaques in this necklace and their very early nineteenth-century style indicate that these mosaics may also have been made by Antonio Aguatti.

68

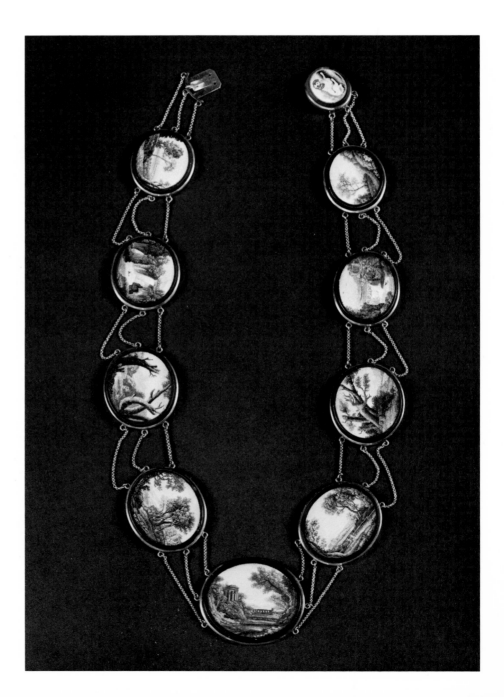

38. Antonio Aguatti, attributed to
Rome, active first half 19th century
Center Table with Cupid in a Chariot
Mosaic, gilt bronze
Diameter: 28⅜ in. (72 cm.)
Height of table: 36½ in. (92.7 cm.)
Promised Gift (G 130)

Collections: Spanish royal family; Jacques Kugel, Paris.

Exhibitions: LACMA, no. 35; LACMA, *Decade*, catalog no. 83, p. 194, repr. in color p. 88.

This gilt-bronze stand has a circular top supported by eight pilasters carrying paired colonnettes with stylized Corinthian capitals. The supports rise from an octagonal base with a mirror in the center that reflects another mirror under the mosaic top. The apron is decorated with applied stylized leaves. The mosaic top shows Cupid in a chariot drawn by tigers surrounded by a wreath of ivy. The mosaic is unsigned but there is a very similar round top in the Hermitage[1] that is signed "Aguatti," most likely Antonio Aguatti (see cat. no. 35). This center table is a fine specimen of its kind. The bronze work is almost certainly French and dates, like the mosaic, to about 1820–25.

69

1. Efimova, *Mozaika,* pp. 10, 99, pl. 48.

39. **Box with a Fox Devouring a Pheasant**
Rome, late 18th–early 19th century
Mosaic, silver gilt
Diameter: 4 in. (10.2 cm.)
Depth of box: 1⅜ in. (3.5 cm.)
Maker's mark: CR WS (Charles Rawlings and
William Summer)
Lion passant: hallmark for Sterling Standard
Capital *C*: letter date for 1840–41
Promised Gift (G 217)

Collection: J. H. Bourdon-Smith, London.

This round Roman mosaic plaque of a fox devouring a pheasant is similar to one in the Hermitage that differs only in the landscape. E. Efimova[1] has attributed the mosaic in the Hermitage to Giacomo Raffaelli. Since it does not appear to be signed this attribution might be questioned, although the period of the mosaic corresponds to that in which Raffaelli was active in Rome, the late eighteenth century to 1804, when he left for Milan. G. A. Guattani notes that Antonio Borghese made a mosaic with a fox and a mallard duck.[2] This is, however, inadequate evidence upon which to ascribe the Gilbert mosaic to Borghese, especially since the bird here appears to be a pheasant. Possibly more substantial is the comment by Gerspach[3] that among the objects made in Paris by the Roman Belloni was a clock decorated with a plaque showing a fox eating a pheasant.

1. Efimova, *Mozaika*, pp. 11, 101, pl. 56.

2. Guattani, *Memorie*, vol. IV, p. 156.

3. E. Gerspach, "Les Mosaïques de Belloni," *Gazette des beaux-arts*, Ser. II, vol. XXXVII, 1888, p. 59.

Monumental Silver: Selections from the Gilbert Collection

Errata

Page

9   column 3, line 19
953.3 should read 958.3

26   column 2, line 1
second should read third

27   column 2, paragraph 2
omit last two sentences

36   column 2, line 3
a baron's should be an earl's

43   De Lamerie illustration should be

50   paragraph 6, line 5
Francis should read Francine

56   column 2
insert heading: Crests before last sentence

87   footnote 2, line 5
ormulu should read ormolu

101   footnote 1, add:
for William IV had assumed
the throne by May of 1821.

Addenda

Catalog

40. Filippo Puglieschi
Rome, active early 19th century
Box with a Dog and Cat Fighting, ca. 1805
Mosaic, gold
Height: 2⁹/₁₆ in. (6.5 cm.)
Width: 3¾ in. (9.5 cm.)
Depth of box: ¾ in. (2 cm.)
Hallmarks: unidentified
Promised Gift (G 151)

Collection: La Vieille Russie, New York.

Exhibitions: LACMA, no. 52c (8); V & A, no. 98.

Literature: Guattani, *Memorie,* vol. II, p. 90.

This rectangular box has a fine scroll decoration on the lid, base, and sides. The marks are unknown, perhaps Piedmontese; one of them, the head of an old man with the letters *s* and *p*, is similar to one used in that region between 1803 and 1809.[1] The mosaic plaque depicts a dog and a cat fighting, with a tree and a landscape in the background.

In 1805 or 1806 Giuseppe Antonio Guattani described the mosaic workshop of Filippo Puglieschi in Rome, where more than 450 pieces including jewelry, boxes, and pictures were being made to fill an order from the north. He commented specifically on a "box cover which he found very beautiful... As to that more amusing than frightening war between the dog and the cat, because of its being originally so well conceived and represented by the incomparable Peters, everyone is as delighted to see it, most especially in mosaic, as they are to see the Capitoline doves."[2]

The "Peters" referred to is Wenceslaus Peter (1742–1829),[3] a celebrated animal painter from Karlsbad in Bohemia, who was active in Rome from 1774 until his death. His pictures were eagerly bought by the Roman nobility, including his patron Prince Marcantonio Borghese.[4] Typical of Peter's work are a lion fiercely attacking a goat, signed and dated 1783, and the lion that served as the model for a mosaic by Michelangelo Barberi for the Villa Demidoff di S. Donato near Florence.[5] They demonstrate the very same taste in subject matter and type of landscape background as the mosaic on the Gilbert box. There seems to be little doubt that the mosaic of a dog and cat fighting that Guattani cites in his account of Puglieschi's mosaic workshop is the one in the Gilbert Collection.

71

1. A. Bargoni, "I punzoni dell'oro e dell'argento in Piemonte durante l'epoca francese (1798–1814)," *Civiltà del Piemonte,* Turin, 1975.

2. Guattani, *Memorie,* vol. II, p. 90.

3. Thieme–Becker, *Künstler Lexikon,* vol. XXVI, 1932, p. 477. For other paintings by Peter, see *Memorie per le Belle Arti,* vol. II, Rome, 1786, p. CXI; Guattani, *Memorie,* vol. IV, p. 146. *Il Settecento a Roma,* exhibition catalog, 1959, p. 172.

4. F. Noack, "Kunstpflege und Kunstbesitz der Familie Borghese," *Repertorium für Kunstwissenschaft,* vol. L, 1929, p. 222, text and fn. 78 (further bibliography). In the entrance hall of the Villa Borghese, Peter painted 162 animals.

5. Reproduced in M. A. Barberi, *Alcuni Musaici usciti dallo studio del Cav. r Michel'angelo Barberi,* Rome, 1856.

41. Filippo Puglieschi, attributed to
Rome, active early 19th century
Panther Attacking a Kid
Mosaic, gilt bronze
Diameter: 3⅞ in. (7.3 cm.)
Promised Gift (G 204)

This round Roman mosaic plaque of a panther attacking a kid in a landscape is set in a gilt-bronze frame crowned by an eagle. In his description of Filippo Puglieschi's workshop in Rome in 1805 or 1806,[1] Guattani noted a mosaic plaque with a panther and a kid after a model by the painter Wenceslaus Peter (1742–1829). This plaque was larger than ours, about 50 by 35 cm., but it must be remembered that Puglieschi also made mosaics as pictures and box covers, and for other decorative purposes. It is more than likely that he used the same cartoon for plaques in various measurements. We can safely attribute the Gilbert plaque to him as it has much in common with cat. no. 40, which is certainly by Puglieschi.

72

1. Guattani, *Memorie,* vol. II, p. 90. In Italian a "pantera" is an Asiatic leopard with larger spots than the African leopard.

42. Filippo Puglieschi, attributed to
Rome, active early 19th century
Box with an Owl Attacking a Kid
Mosaic, tortoiseshell, gold
Height: 2¾ in. (6.9 cm.)
Width: 3½ in. (9 cm.)
Depth of box: 1 in. (2.5 cm.)
City stamp for Paris, 1819–38
Maker's mark: unidentified
m.77.1.72 (G 126)

Collection: Graus, London.

Exhibitions: LACMA, no. 52c (9); V & A, no. 91.

The gold frames and finishings of this tortoiseshell box lined in gold bear the Paris hallmarks used from 1819 to 1838 and an unidentified goldsmith's mark. The mosaic plaque shows an owl attacking a kid. The model for the owl was employed for another plaque in the Gilbert Collection (G 203) where this rapacious bird is devouring a dove. The fine quality of these two plaques is worthy of any of the best mosaicists active in Rome at the beginning of the nineteenth century. Indeed, this mosaic has much in common with those by Filippo Puglieschi in the Gilbert Collection (cat. nos. 40, 41) and also reflects the style of the animal painter Wenceslaus Peter who was responsible for the models of many of Puglieschi's mosaics. Even though no specific documentation has been found, this plaque can be convincingly attributed on stylistic grounds to the Puglieschi-Peter collaboration.

73

The view of the Campagna on this rectangular mosaic opens to the right, with an ancient ruin and three trees to the left. The artist has not been identified, but the style is that of the beginning of the nineteenth century.

74

44. **Temple of the Sibyl at Tivoli**
Rome, early 19th century
Mosaic
7½ x 9⅝ in. (19 x 24.5 cm.)
Promised Gift (G 224)

Collection: Giacomo and Tina Vivanti, Rome.

The Temple of the Sibyl at Tivoli was a "must" for every visitor to Rome in the eighteenth and nineteenth centuries. It was therefore a favorite subject for mosaics of all types (see cat. nos. 19 and 47.) This view of the temple and cascade was produced in a private Roman workshop at the beginning of the nineteenth century.

75

45. Panoramic View of Rome

Rome, early 19th century

Roman mosaic

20⅛ x 52¾ in. (51.1 x 134.3 cm.)

Inscribed, lower left: HINC SEPTEM DOMINOS
VIDERE MONTES ET TOTAM LICET AESTIMARE
ROMAN.

Promised Gift (G 46)

Collections: Sangiorgi, Rome.

Exhibitions: LACMA, no. 19; V & A, no. 18.

Literature: Sherman, *Gilbert*, pp. 34–35, repr. in
color pl. XV.

This Roman mosaic is a faithful copy of the engraving *Prospetto dell'alma città di Roma dal Monte Gianicolo* of 1765 by Giuseppe Vasi (1710–1782).[1] It shows a panoramic view of the city from the height of the Janiculum with the rear of the Palazzo Corsini and its elegant gardens in the center foreground. Vasi's enormous engraving (102 x 264 in.) is dedicated to the king of Spain, Charles III. The Gilbert mosaic duplicates Vasi's view but omits the arms of Charles III at the center and the figure of the Tiber near the she-wolf with Romulus and Remus to the left and adds instead people dressed in folk costume dancing and lying on the grass. These figures are probably derived from Bartolomeo Pinelli (1781–1835). On the large stone slab at the left, where Vasi had put the name of the Spanish king, are inscribed verses from an epigram by Martial: "From here one can see the seven lordly mountains and survey all Rome." This inscription appears on the border of Vasi's view.

Although its dimensions and quality make this view of Rome one of the most striking examples of early nineteenth-century Roman mosaics, it is not signed and does not seem to be mentioned by the sources of the period. It was listed with Messrs. Sangiorgi, Rome, as having been made by a certain Antonio Testa, a name not recorded in the art directories.

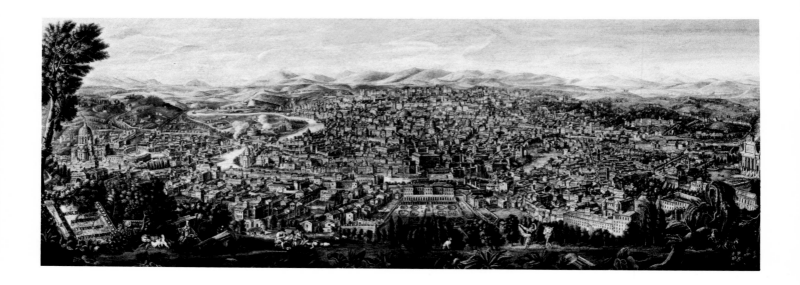

1. A. P. Frutaz, *La pianta di Roma,* Roma; Istituto di studi romani, 1962, vol. I, p. 239, and vol. III, pls. 434–38.

46. Box with a River Landscape

Rome, early 19th century

Mosaic, gold

Height: 2⅜ in. (6 cm.)

Width: 3⅜ in. (8.5 cm.)

Depth of box: ¾ in. (2 cm.)

Maker's mark: indistinct

Paris tax mark for 1809–19

Promised Gift (G 192)

Collection: Le Vieux Paris, Los Angeles.

This rectangular gold box has floral and foliage decoration and a Roman mosaic showing a river landscape with figures in the foreground and a view of a hill town in the left background. The box has lightly-struck Paris tax marks from the years 1809 to 1819.

47. **Box with the Temple of the Sibyl at Tivoli**
Rome, 1819–38
Mosaic, gray granite, silver gilt
Height: 2⅜ in. (6.1 cm.)
Width: 3¼ in. (8.3 cm.)
Depth of box: 1¼ in. (2 cm.)
City stamp for Paris, 1819–38
m.77.1.37 (G 82)

Collection: Richard Ogden, Ltd., London.

Exhibition: V & A, no. 73.

78

This Roman mosaic shows the Temple of the Sibyl at Tivoli. The silver-gilt mounts bear the Paris hallmark for 1819–38, which corresponds to the style of the mosaic and of the box. The view of the temple and waterfall is the same as that used in cat. no. 44, but the composition is less dramatic, the components more stylized.

48. Giovanni Morelli
Lombardy, active early 19th century
Landscape with Castle and Town,
ca. 1820
Mosaic
15¼ x 11¾ in. (38.7 x 29.8 cm.)
Signed, lower left: Gio. Morelli Fece 1820
m.77.1.42 (G 88)

Collection: Antique Lovers Coterie, London.

Exhibitions: LACMA, no. 7; V & A, no. 21.

A landscape view of a hill town appears in the background of this mosaic plaque; two peasants are shown near a waterfall in the lower left foreground. It is signed by Giovanni Morelli,[1] a mosaicist and sculptor who was a pupil of Giocomo Raffaelli in Milan in 1804. Ten years later he was awarded a prize for his mosaic representing St. Jerome. Other of his works are in Paris, London, and Leningrad.

1. Thieme–Becker, *Künstler Lexikon,* vol. XXV, 1931, p. 135–36.

49. **Casket with Playing Putti**
Rome, early 19 century
Mosaic, gilt bronze
Height: 5⅞ in. (15 cm.)
Width: 9⅜ in. (23.8 cm.)
Depth of casket: 5½ in. (13 cm.)
Promised Gift (G 185)

Collection: Grand Duchess Olga von Württemberg; Jacques Kugel, Paris.

Eight small mosaic ovals representing putti playing are set into the repoussé decorations of this rectangular gilt-bronze casket. A ninth oval medallion in mosaic serves to conceal the lock; on the top is a rectangular mosaic panel with a landscape. The mosaics were obviously made in Rome and then incorporated into this casket in Russia, about 1825. Both the workmanship and style of the casket confirm the tradition that it belonged to the daughter of Czar Nicholas I, the Grand Duchess Olga von Württemberg (1822–1892).

50. S. Morelli
Rome, active first half 19th century
Box with Waterfall, Ruins, and a Swan,
ca. 1820
Pietre dure, gold
Height: 3 in. (7.6 cm.)
Width: 3¾ in. (9.5 cm.)
Depth of box: 1⅞ in. (4.7 cm.)
Signed, lower right: S. MORELLI VIA DELLA
SCROFA N. 8.
Maker's mark of Gabriel-Raoul Morel
City stamp of Paris, 1819–38
Promised Gift (G 219)

Collection: S. J. Phillips, Ltd., London.

Exhibition: *Fanfare for Europe,* Britain's Art Market, 1975, no. 294.

The lid of this nearly heart-shaped agate box has gold mounts engraved with a scroll-and-leaf decoration. The agate top itself is encrusted with pietre dure forming in relief a landscape with a swan. An inscription below, partly covered by the gold mount, reads "S. Morelli via della Scrofa N.8." The street referred to is in Rome, and the style of the inscription is purely neoclassical, indicating that the stone was worked by an Italian active in Rome during the late eighteenth or more likely the early nineteenth century. There is no known record of the artist S. Morelli, although a Gio. Morelli, possibly connected with him, signed and dated the *Landscape with Castle and Town* (cat. no. 48) in 1820.

The gold mounts have a Paris hallmark used between 1819 and 1838 and the mark of the goldsmith Gabriel-Raoul Morel, whose shop was at 5 place Thionville. The type of encrustation work in this piece demonstrates that, contrary to previous opinion, such work was not exclusive to Germany—specifically to the workshop of B. G. Hoffman, active in Dresden about the mid-eighteenth century—but can be found in Italy as well.

81

51. **Box with Italian Peasants Bowling**
Rome, early 19th century
Mosaic, tortoiseshell, gold
Height: 2⅛ in. (5.4 cm.)
Width: 3⅛ in. (8 cm.)
Depth of box: 1¹/₁₆ in. (2.4 cm.)
m.77.1.65 (G 122)

Collection: Jacques Kugel, Paris.

Exhibitions: LACMA, no. 52d; V & A, no. 87.

82

 Charles Avery has pointed out that this composition derives from an 1816 engraving by Bartolomeo
Pinelli (1781–1835).[1] Other mosaic plaques in the Gilbert Collection (cat. nos. 45, 55, 77) also show
the influence of the graphic work of Pinelli, whose pastoral or village scenes appealed to the popular taste.

 The box has unmarked gold mounts and a gold frame with a garland of oak leaves and acorns—the
heraldic motif of the Chigi family. It may consequently have been made for a member of that family.

1. Avery, V & A, no. 87, p. 9.

52. The Capitoline Doves of Pliny

Rome, early 19th century
Mosaic
5⅞ x 6⅜ in. (14.9 x 16.3 cm.)
Inscribed: MIRABILIS IBI COLUMBA BIBENS, ET
AQUAM UMBRA CAPITIS INFUSCANS. APRICANTUR
ALIAE SCABENTES SESE IN CANTHARI LABRO.
PLIN. LIB. XXXV. CAP. X.
m.77.1.61 (G 108)

Collection: Arthur Davidson, London.

Exhibitions: LACMA, no. 51b; V & A, no. 109.

83

In the eighteenth and nineteenth centuries the *Capitoline Doves of Pliny*[1] was the most popular mosaic preserved from antiquity and the most frequently repeated by mosaicists in small plaques and large pictures or incorporated into jewelry, boxes, and table tops. This small plaque is among the rarer faithful imitations of the Capitoline original in its rectangular form and retaining its mosaic frame. The quotation from Pliny is, however, an addition, not part of the original. The text is found in modern editions of Pliny in Book XXXVII, chap. 184, rather than in Book XXXV, chap. X: "Among these mosaics is a marvellous dove drinking and casting the shadow of its head on the water. Other doves are pluming their feathers in the sun on the lip of a goblet."[2] The history of the Capitoline mosaic is recounted in the entry for cat. no. 28. The Gilbert plaque can be dated on stylistic grounds to the first quarter of the nineteenth century.

1. H. Stuart Jones, ed., *A Catalogue of the Ancient Sculptures Preserved in the Municipal Collections of Rome, by Members of the British School at Rome, I. The Sculptures of the Museo Capitolino...*, Oxford, 1912, p. 143, col. 13a.

2. Plinius Secundus, C., *The Elder Pliny's Chapters on the History of Art*, trans., K. Jex-Blake, introd., E. Sellers, Chicago: Argonaut, 1968, Appendix IX, pp. 222–25.

53. Conspiracy of Catiline

Rome, first quarter 19th century
Mosaic
8⅛ x 15¼ in. (20.7 x 38.7 cm.)
m.77.1.18 (G 27)

Collection: D. Thomas, London.

Exhibitions: LACMA, no. 6; V & A, no. 8.

Literature: Sherman, *Gilbert,* pp. 36–37, repr. in color pl. XVI; Hillier, *Connoisseur,* p. 270, repr. fig. 2.

84

In 63 B.C., Lucius Catiline fomented a conspiracy to overthrow the government which was discovered and made public by Cicero, then consul, in a series of speeches in the Senate. The episode represented in the mosaic is taken from Sallust's political pamphlet *De Catilinae coniuratione* in which he reported the gossip concerning a meeting of the conspirators: "Some there were at that time, who said, that Catiline, when he had ended his speech, and proceeded to administer an oath to his associates, presented them all round with a bowl of human blood mixed with wine; that when they had all tasted and sworn, as is usual in solemn sacrifices, he disclosed his design to them; and that he did this in order to engage them more strictly to mutual faith, as each was privy to the guilt of another in so horrible a fact."[1]

The two figures in the foreground taking the oath in blood and wine are traditionally identified as P. Cornelius Lentulus and Cornelius Cethegus; the one immediately behind them with the band in his hair and his hand raised in an oratorical gesture is Catiline; and the figure next to him who encourages the oath takers to be strong in their resolutions is Quintus Curius. It was through Curius's idle bragging of expected wealth to his lady friend, Fulvia, that the plot was revealed to Cicero.

The composition is ultimately derived from a painting of 1663 by Salvator Rosa in the Casa Martelli in Florence[2] which was engraved by Denan in 1663, by B. Balla Cecchi in 1780, and again by F. Rainaldi in 1798. It is the 1798 engraving, which changed Rosa's vertical composition into a horizontal, frieze-like one,[3] that is the model for the Gilbert mosaic. While it is neither signed nor dated, the mosaic seems on stylistic grounds to have been made in Rome during the first quarter of the nineteenth century.

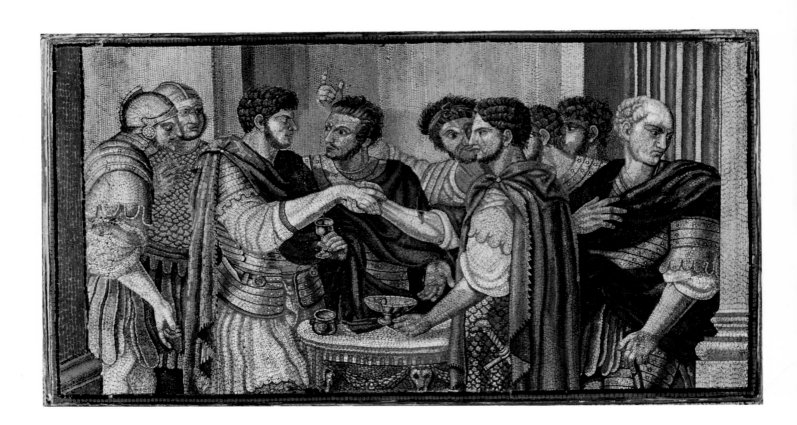

1. C. C. Sallust, *The History of Catiline's Conspiracy...*, trans. W. Rose, London, 1757, p. 21.

2. L. Salerno, *L'opera completa di Salvator Rosa,* Milan: Rizzoli, 1974, pl. 180.

3. Sarasota, Florida, Ringling Museum, *Salvator Rosa: His Etchings and Engravings after His Works,* catalog by P. A. Tomory, 4 November–5 December 1971, no. 54, repr.

54. **Box with Ruins of the Temple of Poseidon, Paestum**

Rome, early 19th century
Mosaic, gold, tortoiseshell, enamel
Height: 2⅜ in. (6.1 cm.)
Width: 3¼ in. (8.3 cm.)
Depth of box: 1 in. (2.5 cm.)
Inscribed, inside: Ruines du Temple de Pestum
Maker's mark of Jean-Louis Lefebvre
m.77.1.48 (G 95)

Collection: S. J. Phillips, Ltd., London.

Exhibitions: LACMA, no. 52b; V & A, no. 79; LACMA, *Decade,* catalog no. 82, p. 194, repr. in color p. 88.

The ruins of Paestum, discovered in the 1740s, had such romantic interest for the eighteenth- and nineteenth-century traveler that great numbers of mosaics of the temple must have been sent from Rome to the north for incorporation into boxes and jewelry. An inscription on the gold inner lining of this box identifies the Roman mosaic on the top as "Ruines du Temple de Pestum." The box, tortoiseshell with gold mounts, some with blue enamel, is French, bearing the marks of the goldsmith Jean-Louis Lefebvre, whose premises were in the rue St. Martin, Paris, at the beginning of the nineteenth century.

The Temple of Poseidon at Paestum shown in the mosaic is the best-preserved of all Greek temples in Italy or Greece. Erected in the early to mid-fifth century B.C., the Doric hexastyle temple is 139¾ feet long and 79½ feet wide. The spectator looks down the center of the interior with fourteen travertine columns 25 feet high and 6 feet in diameter facing the center walls and two rows of seven columns with smaller columns above, which supported the cella roof. The temple was frequently engraved in the eighteenth and nineteenth centuries.

The gold box still has its original red leather case.

55. **Box with S. Paolo fuori le mura after the Fire**
Rome, 1823–25
Mosaic, enamel, gold
Height: 2½ in. (6.4 cm.)
Width: 3⅝ in. (9.2 cm.)
Depth of box: ¾ in. (2 cm.)
Maker's mark of Pierre-André Montauban
Promised Gift (G 238)

Collection: Bulgari, Rome.

This rectangular gold box with blue enamel flowers has marks of the goldsmith Pierre-André Montauban, *maître* in Paris in 1804 and active until about 1825. The mosaic panel shows the interior of the Basilica of S. Paolo fuori le mura, Rome, after it was partly destroyed by fire the nights of 15 and 16 July 1823. The mosaic is based on a drawing by Bartolomeo Pinelli (1781–1835), published by R. Gnoli.[1] This mosaic is a touching memento of the tragic event; visible here are the famous pavonazzetto marble columns of the basilica, the apse with the famous thirteenth-century mosaics of Onofrius III, and the ciborium by Arnolfo di Cambio. Gregory XVI reconstructed the basilica after the fire and restored some of the mosaics. After 1847, Pius IX commissioned a series of 258 medallions in mosaic with the portraits of his predecessors and had the facade of the church redecorated by Nicola Consoni (1814–1884), director of the Vatican Mosaic Workshop. The mosaic portraits were made by Dambrosio, Maldura, Vanutelli, Vecchis, Agricola, Pennachini, Bornia, and Campanile.[2]

86

1. R. Gnoli, *Marmora romana,* Rome: Ed. dell'Elefante, 1971, fig. 185.

2. Gerspach, *Mosaïque,* p. 215. L. de Bruyne, *L'antica serie di ritratti papali della Basilica di S. Paolo fuori le mura,* Rome: Pontificio istituto di archeologia cristiana, 1934.

56. **Perfume Flask**

Rome, ca. 1825

Mosaic, green lava, gold

2⅞ x 1⅝ in. (7.3 x 1.5 cm.)

m.77.1.34 (G 79)

Collection: Antiques Corner, London.

Exhibitions: LACMA, no. 52d; V & A, no. 53.

Literature: Hillier, *Connoisseur,* pp. 272–73, repr. in color.

The flask itself is made of green lava with gold mounts and is embellished with thirteen small Roman mosaic panels with flowers, birds, and views of classical buildings. Still in the neoclassical tradition, this small object must have been made in one of the private workshops in Rome about 1825.

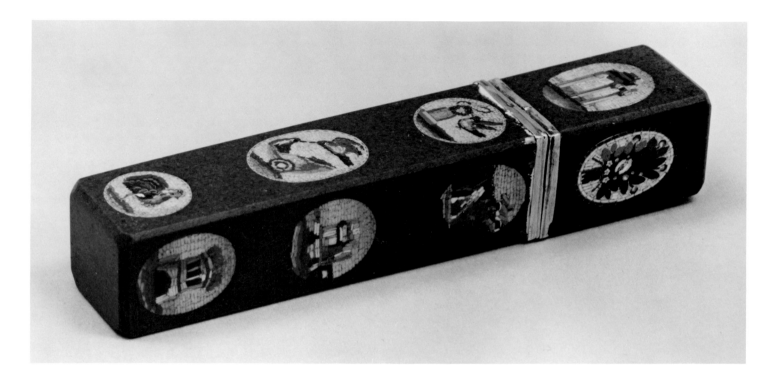

57. **Box with an Anthropomorphic Landscape**
Rome, ca. 1825
Mosaic, tortoiseshell
Diameter: 3¼ in. (8.4 cm.)
Depth of box: ⅞ in. (2.2 cm.)
Inscribed: LE TEMPS QUI DETRUIT TOUT DONNE A
TOUT L'EXISTANCE: DES DEBRIS QUE TU VOIS J'AI
RECU LA NAISSANCE
Promised Gift (G 227)

Collection: Ivano Constantini, Rome.

88

The mosaic lid of this small box displays an anthropomorphic landscape ringed with the inscription: "Le temps qui detruit tout donne a tout l'existance: des debris que tu vois j'ai recu la naissance" (Time which destroys all, gives life to all; from the ruins that you see I came into being.)

The painter Giuseppe Arcimboldo (1527–1593) is the general source for this type of double-image landscape in which the shapes of nature follow the configuration of human forms.[1] In succeeding centuries the idea was borrowed by such engravers as Wenzel Hollar (1607–1677), Joseph Friedrich Leopold (1628–1726), and others of surrealistic bent as late as 1830.[2] One of their engravings, modified and simplified, may have served as the prototype for this piece, which appears to have been made about 1825. No other examples of this type of mosaic are known.

1. B. Geiget, *I dipinti ghiribizzosi di Giuseppe Arcimboldi, pittore, illusionista del cinquecento*, 1527–1593, Florence: Vallecchi, 1954, pls. 19–22. Plate 19, in the collection of Alfred H. Barr, Jr., New York City, is closest to the Gilbert mosaic.

2. E. von Philippovich, *Kuriositäten. Antiquitäten*, Braunschweig: Klinckhart & Bierman, 1966, pp. 23–31, illustrates the engravings. See also F. C. Legrand and Sluys, *Arcimboldo et les arcimboldesques*, Paris: La Nef de Paris, 1955, pls. 51–53.

58. Faustinus Discovering Romulus and Remus
Rome, ca. 1825
Mosaic
Diameter: 2¾ in. (7 cm.)
Promised Gift (G 35)

Collection: Amadeo di Castro, Rome.

Exhibitions: LACMA, no. 48a; V & A, no. 103;
LACMA, *Decade,* catalog no. 82, p. 194, repr. in
color p. 88.

Literature: Sherman, *Gilbert,* pp. 18–19, repr. in
color pl. III; Hillier, *Connoisseur,* p. 272, repr. in
color.

90

In this round mosaic plaque the shepherd Faustinus is shown discovering Romulus and Remus being nursed by the she-wolf on the banks of the Tiber. The river god and three nymphs look on. In the right background is the citadel of Alba Longa, ruled by the usurper Amulius, who had ordered his twin grandnephews drowned to assure that there would be no succession to the line of his elder brother, Numitor. Reared to manhood by Faustinus and his wife, the twins led the shepherds to invade the palace, slay Amulius, and restore Numitor to the throne. They then set out to found the city of Rome on the site of their miraculous rescue.

An almost identical plaque was acquired by the Hermitage in 1928 from the Karabanov Collection. They are obviously Roman and can be dated to about 1825.

1. Efimova, *Mozaika,* pp. 11, 102, pl. 63.

59. **Matched Jewelry Set with Views of Rome**
  Rome, ca. 1825
  Mosaic, glass, gold
  Necklace length: 17½ in. (44.3 cm.)
  Bracelet length: 6¼ in. (15.9 cm.)
  Brooch length: 1¾ in. (4.5 cm.)
  Earring length: 1¾ in. (4.5 cm.)
  City stamp of Paris, 1819–38
  Promised Gift (G 64)

  Collection: Frances Klein, Beverly Hills.

  Exhibitions: LACMA, no. 49; V & A, no. 51.

  Literature: Sherman, *Gilbert,* pp. 24–25, repr. in color pl. VII; Hillier, *Connoisseur,* p. 271, repr. in color fig. 7.

This parure is composed of a necklace, two bracelets, earrings, and a brooch. They include nineteen oval Roman mosaic plaques with views of famous Roman buildings and ruins, all set in light blue glass with gold mounts and filigree decorations. The gold mounts bear the Paris warranty marks for 1819–38, to which the style of the mosaics conforms perfectly. Dating about 1825, the mosaics form an ideal souvenir of Rome, like a series of postcards of great luxury. Among the views on the necklace are the Temple of Vesta, the Tomb of Cecilia Metella, the Temple of Hercules at Cora, the Pantheon, the Forum, the Capitol, the Fontana Paola, the Fontana di Trevi, the Temple of the Sibyl at Tivoli, and the Colosseum. The Temple of Antoninus and Faustina and the Temple of Saturn are on the bracelets; the Piazza S. Pietro on the brooch; and the Temple of Vespasian and the Temple of Castor and Pollux on the earrings.

The jewelry set still has its original red leather case.

60. **Basket with Flowers**
Rome, ca. 1825
Mosaic
2 x 2^{15}/$_{16}$ in. (5 x 7.4 cm.)
m. 77.1.49 (G 96)

Collection: S. J. Phillips, Ltd., London.

Exhibitions: LACMA, no. 516; V & A, no. 106.

This horizontal composition of a mass of flowers in a wide shallow basket is a type frequently used with variation in details by the Vatican Workshop in the first half of the nineteenth century. It was used, for example, in another small mosaic incorporated in a diary in the Gilbert Collection (cat. no. 65); in larger scale on a table top in the Hermitage given by Pope Pius VII to Prince Mikhail Pavlovich;[1] and on another table top given by Pope Leo XII to Count Borommeo in 1825.[2] Stylistically the small Gilbert plaque can be dated to about 1825.

92

1. Efimova, *Mozaika*, pp. 10, 98, pl. 41.

2. A. M. Cito Filormarino, *L'Ottocento, i mobile del tempo dei nonni*, Milan, 1969, pl. 240.

61. Giovanni Battista Luchini
Naples, early 19th century
Pair of Miniatures, 1825–30
Mosaic, gilt copper
Diameter: 1¼ in. (3.2 cm.), each
Signed: Luchini F.
m.77.1.68 (G 123c)
m.77.1.69 (G 123d)

Collection: Jacques Kugel, Paris

Exhibitions: LACMA, no. 52d; V & A, no. 113.

Both of these circular mosaic plaques are signed "Luchini F." One is a portrait of a lady in right profile wearing a tiara and necklace, the other a gentleman in left profile wearing various decorations, including the Golden Fleece. The plaques have traditionally been called Neopolitan and the sitters identified as the Bourbon monarchs Ferdinand I (1751–1825) and Maria Carolina of Austria (1752–1814), king and queen of the Two Sicilies (1815–1825), to whom they bear no likeness whatsoever. They do, however, somewhat resemble Ferdinand's son Francis I (1777–1830) and his queen, Maria Isabella, (d. 1848), daughter of the king of Spain, Charles IV. Francis I succeeded his father in 1825.

While evidence for a precise identification of the artist is lacking, a Giovanni Battista Luchini is registered in the State Archives in Naples as director of a Studio del Mosaico in that city in 1811 and 1814.[1] Drawings for the mosaics were furnished by a Pietro Martorano in 1811; he was not mentioned in 1814. No further documents have yet been discovered indicating how long this mosaic workshop remained active in Naples. This Studio del Mosaico is not to be confused with the Laboratorio delle Pietre Dure in Naples, directed by Antonio Lombardo, which produced works in the Florentine style.

93

1. Archivio di Stato, Naples, Casa Reale Antica 1550, documents concerning January 1811 and June 1814.

62. Matched Jewelry Set

Italy, ca. 1830–40
Mosaic, lapis lazuli, gold
Necklace length: 21 in. (53.3 cm.)
Earring length: 3⅜ in. (8.5 cm.)
Brooch length: 2⅝ in. (6.7 cm.)
Brooch length: 4 in. (10.2 cm.)
m.77.1.78 (G 133)

Collection: S. J. Shrubsole, London.

Exhibitions: LACMA, no. 50; V & A, no. 59.

This elaborate parure consists of a necklace, two brooches, and earrings, with sixteen Roman mosaic plaques of flowers, fruit, birds, and butterflies set in lapis lazuli frames. The gold mounts are Romantic in style and can be dated to about 1830–40; they are possibly Italian.

94

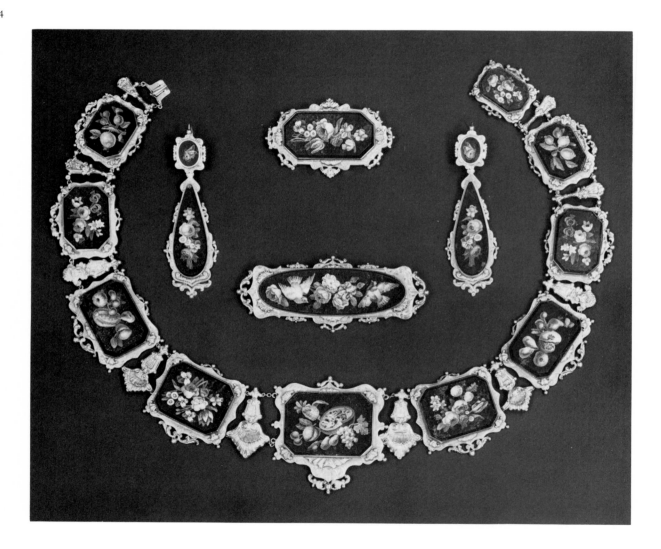

63. Camillo Poggioli
Rome, active first half 19th century
Table Top with Birds, Butterflies, Flowers, and Fruit, 1839
Mosaic, marble
Diameter: 30¾ in. (78 cm.)
Signed: Poggioli f. 1839 in Roma
m. 77.1.31 (G 73)

Collection: G. Constantini, Rome.

Exhibitions: LACMA, no. 41; V & A, no. 37.

The two birds, two butterflies, and four garlands of fruit and flowers of this round mosaic are set in black Belgian marble with a serpentine marble border that bears the signature "Poggioli f. 1839 in Roma." In 1847, G. Moroni[1] mentioned a Camillo Poggioli, unrecorded elsewhere, as being active in Rome as "mosaicista in piccolo," that is, a specialist in mosaics with minute tesserae; he must be the author of the Gilbert table. The four garlands with fruit and flowers are probably symbols of the four seasons: the two with flowers and butterflies representing Spring and Summer; the third with grapes, Autumn; and the fourth with a pomegranate, Winter.

95

1. Moroni, *Dizionario,* vol. XLVII, 1847, p. 80.

64. **Box with a River Landscape**
   Rome, ca. 1840
   Mosaic, gold
   Height: 2⅜ in. (6 cm.)
   Width: 3¼ in. (8.3 cm.)
   Depth of box: 1⅛ in. (2.8 cm.)
   City stamp of Paris after 1838
   Maker's mark of Alexandre Leferre, Paris
   Promised Gift (G 134)

   Collection: Richard Jones, San Diego.

   Exhibitions: LACMA, no. 52d; V & A, no. 94.

    This rectangular gold box has foliage decoration and a Roman mosaic showing a river landscape
with figures. It bears a mark of Alexandre Leferre, registered in Paris before 1806, and a Paris mark used
after 1838. The box can therefore be dated to about 1840.

65. F. Scaccia
Rome, active first half 19th century
Seven-Day Diary,
1841
Mosaic, gold, pigskin
Height: 2¾ in. (7 cm.)
Width: 4⅛ in. (10.5 cm.)
Depth: ½ in. (1.3 cm.)
Signed, lower left: F. Scaccia
Promised Gift (G 171)

Collection: Jacques Kugel, Paris.

     This small mosaic, incorporated into a luxury diary in pigskin with gold mounts, is signed
"F. Scaccia." No record has yet been found of this mosaicist. The composition is of a type employed so
often by the Vatican Workshop (see cat. nos. 27, 60) that it is safe to conclude that it was made there for
export to the north. Two inscriptions on an enclosed notebook read "Semainier de poche, Paris, rue de la
Sorbonne 4" and "1841." The inclusion of the two billing birds among the flowers would have made
this diary an especially suitable gift as an expression of affection.

66. *Benedetto Boschetti*
Rome, active ca. 1820–ca. 1870
Table with Triumph of Cupid,
1823
Mosaic
Diameter: 38½ in. (97.8 cm.)
Height: 32½ in. (82.6 cm.)
Promised Gift (G 100)

Collection: Florence Goldman, New York

Exhibitions: LACMA, no. 37; V & A, no. 39.

One of the nineteenth-century mosaic treasures of the Hermitage[1] is a round table top called "The Triumph of Love." It was made in Rome by Michelangelo Barberi (1787–1867) in 1823, an early work by the man who was to become the leading mosaicist in Rome for the next half-century. Pius VII hoped to buy the table for the Campidoglio but died before the purchase could be completed. Barberi therefore sold the table to Czar Nicholas I during a trip to Russia in 1827. In a book on his mosaics that he published in 1856, Barberi explained the extremely elaborate iconography of his table.[2] He was inspired, he wrote, by Petrarch's description of Amor in his *Trionfo d'amore:*[3]

Vidi un vittorioso e sommo duce	I saw a victorious and exalted leader
pur com'un di color che'n Campidoglio	Quite like one of those who in the Campidoglio
trionfal carro a gran gloria conduce...	drives a triumphal chariot in great glory.
...quattro destrier vie più che neve bianchi;	Four steeds there were, whiter yet than snow,
sovr' un carro di foco un garzon crudo	In the chariot of fire was a cruel youth
con arco in man e con saette a'fianchi;	with bow in hand and arrows at his side;
nulla temea, però non maglia o scudo	Nothing did he fear, therefore he wore neither mail nor shield
ma su gli omeri avea sol due grand'ali	but on his shoulders only two great wings
di color mille, tutto l'altro ignudo...	of a thousand colors, otherwise he was nude.

Around the chariot of Amor in circles joined by chains are the eight planets symbolized by the animals sacred to the ancient gods, whose names the planets bear, and between them the related occupations of man: the ox of Saturn—learned professions; the hound of Diana (Moon)—merchants; the wolf of Mars—military; the eagle of Jupiter—rulers; the ram of Mercury—artisans; the griffin of Apollo—artists; the mare of Ceres (Earth)—farmers; the doves of Venus—poets. These allegorical images represent for Barberi the triumph of love over all the activities of man.

Barberi's table had such great renown that several copies of it were made by distinguished mosaicists in Rome. The Cavaliere Luigi Moglia made one copy that was shown in the Crystal Palace Exhibition in London in 1851 (see cat. no. 80).[4] According to Gaetano Moroni in 1847,[5] Benedetto Boschetti imitated the Barberi table twice. Boschetti, like Moglia, exhibited one of these at the Crystal Palace Exhibition. The official catalog of the exhibition lists: "Two mosaic tables, of 3 feet diameter each, in Byzantine style, representing the Triumph of Love and the Blessed Soul."[6] Since the Gilbert table is signed "B. Boschetti, F. R.," i.e., made by B. Boschetti in Rome, and since the diameter is roughly that of the Crystal Palace table, it is entirely possible that it is the same table. We know from Moroni that the table was made by 1847. It may have been made between 1823 and 1827 when Barberi offered his masterpiece for sale in Rome, but it is also possible that Boschetti had direct access to the original cartoon by the Russian artist F. A. Bruni,[7] after the Barberi table had been shipped to St. Petersburg.

The Gilbert table is a free adaptation of the Hermitage table rather than a literal copy of it. The Amor and his four white horses in the center are more tightly drawn than in the Barberi table, and there is more interest in sculpturesque clarity than in Barberi's painterly burst of light. The Amor is older, the order of the planets has been somewhat altered, the symbols of the occupations have been enlarged and elaborated, and an ivy wreath has replaced the outer border of desiccated leaves. The order of images, clockwise, in the Boschetti table is as follows: the wolf of Mars—rulers; the ox of Saturn—military; the dog of Diana (Moon)—musicians or poets; the eagle of Jupiter—farmers; the ram of Mercury—artisans; the mare of Ceres (Earth)—artists; the griffin of Apollo—merchants; the doves of Venus—learned professions. The theme is the same, but the theoretical unity of the separate parts of the allegory is not maintained.

Little is known of Benedetto Boschetti, although a number of his works have been identified. In 1856, Bonfigli in the *Artistical Directory*[8] lists Boschetti's shop in Via Condotti, no. 74. "The Establishment is particularly conspicuous for its great variety of marble works, bronzes, candelabras, table-tops, etc. besides a rich collection of the best mosaics and shell engravings." He also noted that Boschetti had "attained the Prize Medal at the Exhibition in London." Boschetti is also mentioned in the 1858, 1867 and 1869 editions of Murray's *Handbook.*[9]

Among the works signed "B. Boschetti" and therefore made by Benedetto, who was known primarily as a mosaicist, or by members of his firm, are the following: a vase in giallo antico marble in the collection of Prof. Mario Praz, Rome; a bronze copy of the famous relief of Antinoüs in the Villa Albani, which appeared in a sale in Florence in 1974; a copy in rosso antico marble of the Warwick vase in the Toledo (Ohio) Museum; and a tripod from the Villa d'Iside in Pompeii in the collection of the Knights of Glin, Ireland.[10]

1. Efimova, *Mozaika,* pp. 12, 103, pl. 68, and Efimova, *Barberi,* p. 369ff.

2. *Alcuni Musaici usciti dallo studio del Cav. Michel'angelo Barberi,* Rome, 1856.

3. Francesco Petrarch, *Trionfo d'Amore,* lines 13–27, quoted from F. Petrarch, *Trionfi,* ed. Carlo Calcaterra, Torino, 1927, pp. 5–6.

4. *Official Catalogue of the Great Exhibition of the Works of All Nations,* London, 1851.

5. Moroni, *Dizionario,* vol. XLVII, 1847, p. 80.

6. *Official Catalogue of the Great Exhibition of the Works of All Nations,* London, 1851, p. 1285, no. 17.

7. V. Grigorovich, *Zhurnal izjashnykh iskusstv,* vol. III, no. 6, 1825, pp. 72–74, wrote that the cartoon was designed in Rome by F. A. Bruni. Most nineteenth-century writers believed that Barberi was the author of most of his compositions.

8. F. S. Bonfigli, *Artistical Directory or Guide to the Studios of the Italian and Foreign Painters and Sculptors,* Rome, 1856.

9. Murray, *Handbook,* 1858, 1869 and 1867, p. XXVI, sec. 36.

10. A. Gonzalez-Palocios, "I mani del Piranesi, I Righetti, Boschi, Boschetti, Raffaelli," *Paragone,* no. 315, May 1976, pp. 38–40.

67. Michelangelo Barberi
Rome, 1787–1867
Table with "The Most Beautiful Skies of Italy,"
1846–51
Mosaic, gilt bronze
Diameter: 38⅞ in. (98.7 cm.)
Height: 31½ in. (80 cm.)
m.77.1.81 (G 145)

Collection: Dr. Ricks, Oklahoma City.

Exhibitions: LACMA, no. 38; V & A, no. 44.

Literature: Hillier, *Connoisseur*, pp. 268–69; repr. in color.

In the center of this round Roman mosaic table, grouped together and floating in the open sky, are four genii carrying the attributes of painting, music, architecture, and sculpture. Around the circumference of the table are eight sections with characteristic scenes of important Italian cities, the names of which are inscribed near the rim. Clockwise, these are the Piazza del Duomo, Milan; the Piazza S. Marco, Venice; the Piazza della Signoria, Florence; the Piazza S. Pietro, Rome; the Colosseum, Rome; the Rivera di Chiaia, Naples, with Vesuvius in the background; the church of S. Rosalia, Palermo; and the harbor, Genoa. The scenes are divided by green columns and encircled by an outer border with blue and green fictive jewels and medallions of horses' and stags' heads.

The Gilbert table is closely related to one in the Hermitage ordered by Czar Nicholas I from Michelangelo Barberi in 1846.[1] Barberi described the Hermitage table in a book on his mosaics published in 1856,[2] in which he states that he chose the cities portrayed in the table because they were the ones visited by the czar and czarina during their Italian trip in 1845. Rome is represented by two views since it was the center of the classical world as well as the seat of Christianity. The Hermitage table also has four genii in the center but they hold a portrait of the Czarina, Alexandra Fedorovna. It has a more complex outer frieze than the Gilbert table with reproductions of famous paintings and sculptures symbolizing the scope of Italian genius.

We know that Barberi himself made a second version of the czar's table for Lord Kilmoran and exhibited it at the Crystal Palace Exhibition of 1851.[3] For it he received a Council Medal, the highest honor conferred at the exhibition. In making the award the judges noted the "singular delicacy and beauty of the workmanship, the admirable adaptability of the material to the nature of the work and the style of the design, the exquisite shading of the colours, and the brilliant though softened effect of the group of views, the atmosphere and the sky of each mingling into the same ethereal tint, which relieves the eye, and allows it to rest with pleasure on the separate views."[4] It is reasonable to identify the Gilbert table as the one that received this singular honor: it is the only known table of this design other than that in the Hermitage, and, of even greater importance, it is of a quality indeed worthy of Barberi himself. The gilt-bronze base, consisting of four splayed legs with goats' heads at the top joined by a ring in the center and a cross-shaped element below, is typically Italian of the mid-nineteenth century.

Michelangelo Barberi was regarded by his contemporaries as the most accomplished mosaicist of his day. He was born in Rome on 8 May 1787.[5] A pupil of Antonio Aguatti, he became associated with the Vatican Mosaic Workshop about 1820. His fame was established by his table top of the *Triumph of Love* created in 1823 and sold to Czar Nicholas I in 1827[6] on a visit to Russia. This inaugurated a long relationship with the court at St. Petersburg which culminated in a training program for Russian mosaicists in Rome conducted by Barberi from 1846 to 1850, when the pensionaires accompanied by J. and L. Bonafede from Rome returned to St. Petersburg to set up a mosaic workshop in the Academy of Fine Arts on the model of the Vatican Workshop.[7] During those years Barberi continued to receive commissions from the czar. In addition to the two tables mentioned, there are three other of his tables in the Hermitage: *Twenty-Four Hours in Rome*, 1839; a smaller version, 1843; and *The Monuments of Rome*, 1847.[8] From 1852 to 1854 he executed mosaics for the Villa S. Donato of Prince Demidoff near Florence. Moroni wrote that Barberi also made minute mosaics for jewels inspired by literary and folk subjects. In 1856 he was appointed Commendatore of the Order of S. Silvestro by Pius IX; He is mentioned in the guide books of the 1860s as having an establishment at 148 Via Rasella, and Murray's *Handbook* of 1864 records that "he was director of the mosaic works of the government" but that his health was declining.[9] He died on 7 August 1867.

Barberi's importance to the history of mosaics extends also to technique. He continued the research of his teacher Aguatti and, with the help of his assistant Giuseppe Matta, he was able to reduce the size of tesserae still further than Aguatti and to obtain a greater number of colors simultaneously.[10]

1. Efimova, *Mozaika*, pp. 12, 104–5, pl. 73; Efimova, *Barberi*, pp. 378–79, pl. 6.

2. *Alcuni musaici usciti dallo studio del Cav. Michel'Angelo Barberi*, Rome, 1856.

3. *L'Album*, vol. XXIII, 1856, pl. 210.

4. *Great Exhibition of the Works of the Industry of All Nations, MDCCCLI, Reports by the Juries*, London, 1851, p. 1286.

5. R. Di Stasio Battaglini, "Michelangelo Barberi," *Dizionario biografico degli Italiani*, Rome, 1954, vol. VI, pp. 163–64, with extensive bibliography.

6. Efimova, *Mozaika*, pp. 12, 103; pl. 68; Efimova, *Barberi*, pls. 1–3.

7. Gerspach, *Mosaïque*, pp. 216–18.

8. Efimova, *Mozaika*, pp. 12, 103, 104, pls. 70–72; Efimova, *Barberi*, pls. 4,5,7,8.

9. Murray, *Handbook*, 1864.

10. Moroni, *Dizionario*, vol. XLVII, 1847, p. 79.

68. **Box with a View of Berchtesgaden**

Rome, second quarter 19th century

Mosaic, gold

Height: 2⅝ in. (6.7 cm.)

Width: 3¹⁵⁄₁₆ in. (10 cm.)

Depth of box: 1 in. (2.5 cm.)

Hallmark: unidentified

Promised Gift (G 120)

Collection: Jacques Kugel, Paris

Exhibitions: LACMA, no. 52d; LACMA, *Decade,* catalog no. 82, p. 194, repr. in color p. 88; V & A, no. 85.

Literature: Hillier, *Connoisseur,* pp. 272–73, repr. in color.

102

Pink, yellow, green, and white gold and blue enamel decorate this rectangular gold box, which has a French mark used after 1819. The mosaic shows a mountainous landscape with a river and a hill town. Two nineteenth-century notes[1] in the box when it was acquired for the Gilbert Collection state that this box was presented by King Maximilian I of Bavaria to Marie Philippe Aimé de Golbéry, in appreciation for the gift of a study of the antiquities of Alsace which de Golbéry published in 1825, the year of Maximilian's death. One of the notes is on the back of a calling card of Madame Monnier, née de Golbéry. Stylistically the mosaic seems to this author to be slightly later.

1. Los Angeles County Museum of Art archives.

69. **Box with a View of the Colosseum**
Rome, second quarter 19th century
Mosaic, gold, enamel
Height: 2⅜ in. (6 cm.)
Width: 3⅜ in. (8.6 cm.)
Depth of box: ⅞ in. (2.2 cm.)
Mark: unidentified
m.77.1.73 (G 127)

Collection: Ben Simon, Paris.

Exhibition: LACMA, no. 92; V & A, no. 92.

This rectangular gold box has a floral border and an edging in blue enamel. The marks are
unidentified although they are also found on a box in the Victoria and Albert Museum (M.226.1917).
The maker was probably Swiss and active during the second quarter of the nineteenth century. Since the
Roman mosaic shows the Colosseum as it was before the excavation and reinforcement of the building
was begun by Pius VII in 1805, the view must have been taken from a drawing or print made before
that date.

70. **Clasp with Romulus and Remus**
Rome, second quarter 19th century
Mosaic, malachite, gold
2 x 2½ in. (5.1 x 5.7 cm.)
m.77.1.60 (G 107)

Collection: M. Elstein, London.

Exhibitions: LACMA, no. 49; V & A, no. 57.

The clasp of this bracelet of braided human hair is an octagonal Roman mosaic plaque set in malachite mounted in gold with an elaborate frame of Baroque volutes. The plaque, which depicts Romulus and Remus being suckled by the she-wolf, can be dated to the second quarter of the nineteenth century. The same model, a painting by Rubens in the Capitoline Museum, served for mosaics on two tables in the Hermitage collections:[1] the first table, with malachite veneer, has eight views of Rome and, at the center, a roundel with a mosaic medallion very similar to ours but with some variations in the landscape; the second table has four oval medallions with four seasons around the central plaque of Romulus and Remus, which again has a different landscape background. The artists of the tables and of this mosaic plaque have not been identified.

1. Efimova, *Mozaika,* pp. 12, 105, pls. 74, 75. These tables were acquired by the Hermitage in 1927 and 1960, respectively, and nothing is said of their nineteenth-century provenance.

71. **Three Brooches with Flowers**
Rome, second quarter 19th century
Mosaic, gold
$1^{17}/_{32}$ x 2 in. (4 x 5.1 cm.)
¾ x $^{15}/_{16}$ in. (1.9 x 2.4 cm.)
¾ x $^{15}/_{16}$ in. (1.9 x 2.4 cm.)
Promised Gift (G 178)

The brooches, one large and a pair of smaller ones, are formed from three Roman mosaic plaques with flowers mounted in gold. The style of the mosaic and of the gold mount can be ascribed to the second quarter of the nineteenth century. While many of the mosaics of that period were archaizing, the delicate shading of light and the softness of modeling effect a close resemblance to contemporaneous still-life painting.

Rome, second quarter 19th century
Mosaic
Diameter: 41⅜ in. (105 cm.)
m.75.135.4 (G 5)

Collection: Herbert Trigger, New York.

Exhibition: LACMA, no. 44.

Literature: Sherman, *Gilbert,* p. 47, repr. in color pl. XXIII.

This representation of a basket of flowers with two billing doves is an obvious symbol of love as the spring of life. The work can be dated to the second quarter of the nineteenth century (see cat. nos. 27, 60, and 65 for similar designs). "A mosaic with two pigeons and flowers" was exhibited by a Roman mosaicist, E. Dies, at the Crystal Palace Exhibition in London in 1851.[1]

1. *Great Exhibition,* p. 1287, no. 39.

73. **Table with Views of Rome**
Rome, second quarter 19th century
Mosaic, gilt wood
Diameter: 32⅞ in. (83.5 cm.); with frame,
37¾ in. (95.9 cm.)
Height of table: 28½ in. (72.4 cm.)
m.75.135.15 (G 223)

Collection: Ivano Constantini, Rome

The Roman mosaic top consists of a central roundel with a view of St. Peter's Square that is separated by a Greek-key design border from twelve other panels with views of the best-known ancient Roman buildings, reading clockwise: Temple of the Sibyl at Tivoli; Forum of Nerva with portico and relief of Minerva; Forum of Augustus; Arch of Janus Quadrifrons; Pantheon; Colosseum; Temple of Vesta; Arch of Titus; Forum; Temple of Antoninus and Faustina; Tomb of Cecilia Metella; Campidoglio. The work dates to the second quarter of the nineteenth century, but it is curious to note that the Colosseum is shown as it was before the restoration begun by Pius VII in 1805 while the Pantheon is shown without the belfries that were not torn down until 1883. It can, therefore, be assumed that the mosaicist was working from an old engraving of the Colosseum and a neoclassic engraving of the Pantheon that had already removed the Baroque intrusions. The pedestal of gilt wood is carved to form three entwined dolphins and appears to be of the same date as the top.

74. F. Della Valle
Leghorn, mid-19th century
**Table with Floral Decoration, Birds,
and Butterflies**
Scagliola, ebony, marquetry, mother-of-pearl
Height: 32⅛ in. (81.6 cm.)
Width: 52⅝ in. (133.7 cm.)
Height of table: 33½ in. (85 cm.)
Signed: F. Della Valle
m.77.1.89 (G 201)

Collection: South Audley Art Galleries, London.

Literature: *Great Exhibition,* p. 1300.

Florentine pietre dure work was so costly in materials and man hours that the larger pieces could be acquired only by royalty or the wealthiest of aristocratic patrons. Consequently, in the seventeenth century a less expensive and more easily worked imitation, called scagliola, was invented. Scagliola was made by combining finely ground gypsum with glue, marble, and granite dust to form a plaster that could be worked like stucco but, when set, could be given a high polish like marble.[1]

The scagliola top of this center table has a rich border of vines, leaves, flowers, birds, and cornucopias, and a central cartouche with two birds on a branch of a cherry tree. The branch bears the signature "F. Della Valle." The support is veneered with ebony and inlaid with ivory, mother-of-pearl, and exotic woods, some of which have been artificially tinted. The apron has a marquetry decoration similar to that on the scagliola top. At the corners are carved eagle heads atop the incurvate legs of square section with floral marquetry. At the bottom is a platform base with a rich marquetry of garlands of leaves and flowers encircling butterflies at the center. The feet have the form of tortoises, cast in bronze and coated with gesso and gilt.

This table was exhibited in the Crystal Palace in 1851; the catalog states that the scagliola top was made by the Della Valle brothers, who had a workshop in Leghorn.[2] The woodwork of the table, however, is even more important than the scagliola top. The table can, in fact, be considered one of the best examples of cabinetmaking in Tuscany of the second quarter of the nineteenth century. It can safely be attributed to the Falcini brothers, Luigi and Antonio, who were famous in Florence at the time. Their specialty[3] was the very sort of marquetry used in the Gilbert table, inspired by famous seventeenth-century prototypes and fabricated of ivory, mother-of-pearl, and artificially dyed woods. The Falcinis' works were eagerly collected by the grand seigneurs of the day, including Prince Demidoff. In the 1969 sale of the remains of the Demidoff Collection in the villa of Pratolino, Florence,[4] were four tables very close to the Gilbert table. L. Bandera has convincingly shown[5] that these tables are by the hand of the Falcini brothers. A gouache by Fortuné de Fournier shows two of them in the ballroom of the Villa Demidoff at San Donato, Florence, as early as 1841. Two of the Demidoff tables were bought by the Soprintendenza alle Belle Arti, Florence, and are now in the Palazzo Pitti.

1. E. Neumann, "Materialen zur Geschichte der Scagliola," *Jahrbuch der Kunsthistorischen Sammlungen in Wien,* vol. LV, 1955, pp. 75–158, is an extensive history of scagliola with many illustrations.

2. *Great Exhibition,* p. 1300.

3. D. Finocchietti, *Della scultura e tarsia in legno,* Florence, 1873, p. 212ff.

4. *Catalogo di quanto e contenuto nella villa Demidoff a Pratolino, presso Firenze . . . venduto . . . da Sotheby's of London.,* 21–24 April 1969.

5. L. Bandera, "Due ebanisti per il Principe Demidoff," *Arte illustrata,* no. 17/18, May 1969, pp. 66ff.

75. **Still Life: Basket of Fruit and Flowers**
Rome, mid-19th century
Mosaic
22⅝ x 17½ in. (57.4 x 44.4 cm.)
m.75.135.1a (G 1a)

Collection: Florence Goldman, New York.

Exhibitions: LACMA, no. 21; V & A, no. 1

Literature: Sherman, *Gilbert,* p. 23, repr. in color
pl. VI.

76. Still Life: Vase of Flowers
Rome, mid-19th century
Mosaic
24⁵/₁₆ x 21⅜ in. (61.8 x 54.3 cm.)
m.75.135.1b (G 1b)

Collection: Florence Goldman, New York.

Exhibitions: LACMA, no. 22; V&A, no. 2.

Literature: Sherman, *Gilbert*, p. 22, repr. in color
pl. V.

Although framed as a pair, the two pictures are different in subject and original format. No. 75 is square and depicts a basket of fruit and flowers, with a bird and butterfly hovering above and with a pond of fish below. No. 76 is oval, with an elaborate vase containing a bouquet of flowers set on a ledge. Both compositions derive from Baroque prototypes. The vase of flowers follows a design popular in both Netherlandish and Italian painting of the second half of the seventeenth century, typical examples of which are found in the works of the Florentine A. Scacciati, designer of pietre dure and marquetry for Cosimo III. This pair of still lifes with their original gilt-wood frames can be dated to about the middle of the nineteenth century.

77. **Jewelry Set with Figures**
Rome, mid-19th century
Gold, mosaic, glass
Bracelet length: 7¾ in. (19.7 cm.)
Brooch length: 2⅛ in. (5.4 cm.)
Earring length: 1⅜ in. (3.8 cm.)
Maker's mark: undeciphered
City stamp of Rome *(bollo camerale),* 1815–70
m.77.1.36 (G 81)

Collection: Bernardo Sado, in London.

Exhibition: LACMA, no. 48d; V& A, no. 54.

Literature: Hillier, *Connoisseur,* p. 272, repr. in color.

This jewelry set consists of a bracelet, earrings, and a brooch made up of eight oval Roman mosaic plaques set in red glass frames and mounted in gold. The mosaics show figures in peasant dress drawn from or inspired by the graphic work of Bartolomeo Pinelli (1781–1835). The gold has the official mark of Rome *(bollo camerale)* used between 1815 and 1870 and a maker's mark that has not yet been deciphered. The jewelry set still has its original purple velvet box.

This pair of mosaic paintings shows the archeological center of Rome as it appeared in the second quarter of the nineteenth century. No. 78 represents the Colosseum after the restorations of Pius VII and Leo XII; the Fountain of Titus (Meta sudans); and, at right, the Arch of Constantine, all seen from the east entrance of the Roman Forum. No. 79 is a view of the Forum from the slopes of the Capitoline Hill. At left is the arch of Septimus Severus, behind which is visible the pediment and roof of the Curia, the meeting place of the Roman senators. In the foreground center are three Corinthian columns of the Temple of Vespasian, built by Domitian in A.D. 81. Further to the right are the eight Doric columns of the Temple of Saturn. Beyond the Temple of Saturn, in the center of the Forum, is the last honorary monument erected in the Forum: the tall column dedicated to the Byzantine emperor Foca in A.D. 608. At the far end of the Forum is the Arch of Titus and to the left are the church of Sta. Francesca Romana and the Colosseum.

116

Both paintings are signed "Moglia F." on the lower left border. In the official catalog of the Crystal Palace Exhibition in London, two mosaics of similar description are listed under the name "Moglia, Domenico."[1] Moroni in 1847[2] identified the mosaicist Domenico Moglia (1780–ca. 1862) as the father of the more famous Cavaliere Luigi Moglia. Both father and son worked in Rome. Domenico's masterpiece is the mosaic portrait of George IV in the Brighton Museum, after a painting by Thomas Lawrence. It is signed and dated 1829. The Roman Domenico Moglia is not to be confused with the well-known Milanese designer of the same name.

1. *Great Exhibition,* p. 1286.
2. Moroni, *Dizionario,* LXVII, 1847, p. 80.

79. Domenico Moglia
   Rome, 1780–ca. 1862
   The Roman Forum,
   ca. 1850
   Mosaic
   18¾ x 25⅞ in. (46.7 x 65.7 cm.)
   Signed, lower left border: MOGLIA F.
   Promised Gift (G 209)

   Collections: Jade Hill, New York

   Exhibition: *Great Exhibition,* p. 1286, no. 21.

80. Luigi Moglia
Rome, active mid-19th century
Lavinia as Flora
Mosaic
14 3/5 x 12 in. (135.5 cm. x 30.5 cm.)
Signed, lower right border: L. MOGLIA, F.
Promised Gift (G 109)

Collection: Fairclough, London.

Exhibition: LACMA, no. 5; V & A, no. 24.

118

An example of the most accomplished craftsmanship, this Roman work is a translation into mosaic of Titian's *Girl with a Bowl of Fruit,* which in the nineteenth century was believed to be a portrait of the artist's daughter, Lavinia, as Flora. The painting, now in the State Picture Gallery, Berlin, Dahlem, was in Florence until 1832, in the collection of the Abate Celotti, where the mosaicist could have seen it.

Luigi Moglia, who signed this mosaic, was so highly esteemed as a mosaicist that he was given the rank of Cavaliere. F. S. Bonfigli reported in *The Artistical Directory* of 1856[1] that Luigi Moglia lived at 134 Via del Babuino, where a variety of his mosaics were to be seen, and that he had been awarded a medal at the Crystal Palace Exhibition of 1851 in London. Moglia did, in fact, exhibit a number of mosaics at the Crystal Palace[2] which exemplify the scope of his work: *The Temples of Paestum, The Pantheon* (2 mosaics), *The Colosseum, The Temple of the Sibyl at Tivoli, The Piazza of St. Peter's in Rome, Wild Boar Hunt, St. George,* two figures after Carlo Dolci, and a copy of Michelangelo Barberi's *Triumph of Love* (see cat. no. 65). Murray's *Handbook* of 1858 and 1867[3] says of him: "Cav. Luigi Moglia, via Babuino 133, is a first rate artist—his Madonna della Seggiola, recently purchased by the Emperor of the French,[4] of the same size as the original picture by Raphael, in the Pitti Gallery, is one of the finest specimens of modern mosaics— his Temples of Paestum obtained one of the Council medals at the London Exhibition in 1851." The 1869 edition of the same *Handbook* states that Cav. Luigi Moglia was then living on Via di S. Maria in via Lata and adds to the list of his works a copy of Guido Reni's *Aurora* in the Rospigliosi Palace. To this list should be added a fine portrait of Gregory XVIII, signed and dated 1838, in the Hermitage.[5]

1. F. S. Bonfigli, *The Artistical Directory, or Guide to the Studios of the Italian and Foreign Painters and Sculptors Resident in Rome,* Rome, 1856.

2. *The Art Journal Illustrated Catalog. The Industry of All Nations,* London: G. Virtue, 1851, p. 1287, nos. 20, 40–45.

3. Murray, *Handbook,* 1867, p. XXVI, section 36.

4. Today in the Musée du Second Empire, Compiègne. Another copy of the Madonna della Seggiola is in the Sala degli Ambasciatori of the Palazzo del Quirinale.

5. Efimova, *Mozaika,* pp. 11, 102, pl. 62.

81. Luigi Moglia
Rome, active mid-19th century
Brooch with Madonna del dito
Mosaic, garnets, turquoise, gilt brass
1¾ x 1⅜ in. (4.4 x 3.5 cm.)
Signed, left side: L. MOGLIA
Promised Gift (G 78)

Collection: Antique Lovers Coterie, London.

Exhibitions: LACMA, no. 52a; V & A, no. 52.

Literature: Hillier, *Connoisseur,* pp. 272–73, repr. in color.

This oval Roman mosaic, signed "L. Moglia," is a faithful copy of the *Madonna del dito,* named for the tip of the finger that protrudes from her garment, by the Florentine painter Carlo Dolci (1616–1686).[1] Like the Titian *Lavinia as Flora,* the *Madonna del dito* was in Florence in the early nineteenth century and could have been copied there by the mosaicist. Carlo Dolci was the ideal *Christianus pictor,* whose aim was to stimulate spiritual fervor through his paintings. His works became the most popular devotional images of Catholicism and were frequently reproduced in many media.

That this mosaic was considered to be especially precious is indicated by its frame of gilt brass with a rich decoration of a wreath of flowers, leaves, and cabochons of turquoise and garnets.

119

1. Florence, Galleria Pitti, no. 206.

82. Luigi Moglia, attributed to
Rome, active mid-19th century
The Pantheon
Mosaic
18 x 22½ in. (45.7 x 57.1 cm.)
m.77.1.21 (G 32a)

Collection: Piero Di Nepi, Rome.

Exhibitions: LACMA, no. 9; V & A, no. 10.

Literature: Sherman, *Gilbert*, p. 31, repr. in color
pl. XIII.

120

This rectangular Roman mosaic represents the Piazza della Rotonda in Rome as it appeared in the mid-nineteenth century. The Pantheon still has "Bernini's donkey ears," the belfries probably erected by Giovanni Lorenzo Bernini under Urban VIII and demolished in 1882. At the left is the fountain to which Clement XI added an Egyptian obelisk from the nearby temple of Isis in 1711. The mosaic can be dated on stylistic grounds to the second quarter of the nineteenth century.

Among the mosaics shown in the Crystal Palace Exhibition of 1851 were two views of the Pantheon by Luigi Moglia.[1] The quality of the Gilbert Pantheon is worthy of that master and may indeed be one of those included in the London exhibition.

1. *Great Exhibition*, p. 1287, nos. 33, 44.

83. **Souvenir of Rome**
Rome, mid-19th century
Mosaic
8½ x 11½ in. (21.6 x 28.6 cm.)
Inscribed, center foreground: Ricordo di Roma
m.77.1.19 (G 28)

Collection: S. Lewis, London.

Exhibitions: LACMA, no. 15; V & A, no. 9.

Literature: Sherman, *Gilbert,* p. 26 , repr. in color
pl. VIII.

At the center of this oval mosaic is a fountain; to the left is a moonlight view of the Colosseum with an opalescent mother-of-pearl moon; to the right is a daytime view of St. Peter's Square. On a plaque in the foreground is written: "Ricordo di Roma" (Souvenir of Rome). The Colosseum is depicted as it appeared after the restoration made under Pius VII. This, and the fashion in which the figures are dressed, implies a date toward the middle of the last century. Throughout the nineteenth century the Colosseum by moonlight had a strong romantic attraction to tourists, memorialized by Henry James in *Daisy Miller.* The poetic idea of representing Rome both by day and by night may have derived from two of the views inserted in a table by Michelangelo Barberi of 1846–47, which is now in the Hermitage.[1]

1. Efimova, *Mozaika,* pp. 12, 104, pl. 72.

84. Georgii Wekler
St. Petersburg, 1800–1861
Two Whippets,
1853
Mosaic
4 $\frac{5}{32}$ x 5¾ in. (10.5 x 14.6 cm.)
Signed, bottom right: G. WEKLER, 1853
m.77.1.63 (G 115)

Collection: J. J. Szymanski, Beverly Hills.

Exhibition: V & A, no. 25.

Literature: Hillier, *Connoisseur,* p. 270, fig. 3.

This rectangular mosaic of two whippets in a landscape is signed at bottom right, "G. Wekler, 1853." Georgii Wekler or Weckler[1] was born in Riga in 1800 and moved to St. Petersburg the following year. At the age of fourteen he was apprenticed to the Roman mosaicist Mollie (Moglia?) and worked first in St. Petersburg, then from 1817–1819 in Moscow, and accompanied him to Rome. Upon his return to St. Petersburg in 1821, his mosaic paintings so impressed Czar Alexander I that in 1822 he was named "master mosaicist" at the Academy of Arts. He was highly lauded by both Czars Alexander I and Nicholas I for his mosaic copies of paintings in the Hermitage. In 1834 he was awarded a royal pension to work in Rome. From April 1835 to May 1837 he made a full-size copy of Raphael's *Transfiguration,* which was considered one of the technical achievements of the time and for which he was awarded a gold medal by the pope. Following his return to St. Petersburg, Wekler was made "Court master mosaicist" and on March 16, 1838, a member of the Academy. According to Nagler he was appointed director of the mosaic workshop of the grandiose St. Isaacs' Cathedral in St. Petersburg in 1842.[2] In addition to monumental mosaics, Wekler produced small mosaics of city views, landscapes, and animals, like the Gilbert *Two Whippets,* which were eagerly sought by the Russian court and aristocracy. The painting that served as a model for the *Two Whippets* may have been made by an artist of the preceding generation.

1. G. K. Nagler, *Neues allgemeines Künstler-Lexikon,* 2nd ed., vol. XXIV, 1913, pp. 15–18.

2. Thieme-Becker, *Künstler Lexikon,* vol. XXXV, 1942, p. 238.

85. Liberato Aureli (?)
Rome, active 1854–1865
Bracelet with Flowers
Mosaic, gold
Length: 7¼ in. (18.4 cm.)
City stamp of Rome *(bollo camerale),* 1815–70
Maker's mark of Liberato Aureli (?)
m.77.1.52 (G 99)

Collection: D. and J. Welby Antiques, London.

Exhibitions: LACMA, no. 50; V & A, no. 56.

124

    This bracelet is composed of five oval Roman mosaic plaques, each with a bouquet of flowers set in black glass, mounted in gold decorated with filigree. The gold has the hallmark of the city of Rome *(bollo camerale),* which was in use from 1815 until 1870,[1] and a maker's mark which, although very difficult to decipher, could be that of Liberato Aureli, who was active in Rome from 1854 to 1865 and had a shop on Via dei Sabini, no. 6.[2]

1. C. Bulgari, *Argentieri, gemmari e orafi d'Italia,* Rome: Lorenzo del Turco, vol. I, Rome, 1958, p. 32.

2. *Ibid.,* p. 82.

86. Rossi
Rome, active late 19th century
View of Rome,
1870
Mosaic
7½ x 10 in. (19 x 25.4 cm.)
Signed, lower right border: Rossi Roma 1870
Promised Gift (G 155)

Collection: Hancocks & Co., London.

This oval mosaic with a view of the Ponte Rotto and the Isola Tiberina, Rome, is signed "Rossi Roma 1870." Attempts to identify this mosaic artist have been unsuccessful to date.

87. L. A. Gallandt
Rome, active third quarter 19th century
The Roman Forum
Mosaic
34 x 65 in. (86.3 x 165.1 cm.)
Signed, lower right: L. A. Gallandt
m.77.1.82 (G 146)

Collection: Florence Goldman, New York.

Exhibitions: LACMA, no. 17; V & A, no. 31.

To the left of the Roman Forum in this mosaic appear the Baroque church of SS. Luca e Martina, the Temple of Vespasian, and the Arch of Septimius Severus; in the center, the Temple of Saturn; in the distance, the Colosseum, the church of S. Francesca Romana, and the Arch of Titus; in the mid-distance to the right, the three columns of the Temple of Castor and Pollux, and the church of S. Maria Antiqua, above which is the Palatine. The mosaic is signed "L. A. Gallandt." Little is known about this mosaicist; Gerspach mentions a "Monsieur Galland" who produced the models for some of the mosaic decoration of the Pantheon in Paris.[1] Judging by the state of the excavations and the style of the Gilbert mosaic he must have been active during the third quarter of the nineteenth century.

1. Gerspach, *Mosaïque*, p. 234.

88. Table with Arabs Hunting

Rome, third quarter 19th century
Mosaic, marble
Diameter: 35 7/16 in. (90 cm.)
Height of table: 31 in. (78.8 cm.)
m.75.135.13 (G 31)

Collection: Studio del Mosaico, Vatican.

Exhibitions: LACMA, no. 40; V & A, no. 33.

Literature: Sherman, *Gilbert,* pp. 44–45, repr. in color pl. XXI.

128

Both the central scene of three Arabs hunting a lioness and the border of morning glories are in Roman mosaic on black Belgian marble. The label on the reverse reads "Studio del Musaico. Rev. Fabbrica S. Pietro. No. 4552A, Scena di caccia araba" (Arab Hunting Scene). The composition, a typical product of the Vatican Mosaic Workshop during the third quarter of the nineteenth century, is akin to the style of Horace Vernet (1789–1863), who had considerable influence on Roman and other European painters of the period. The table top still has its original pedestal base with lion's paw tripod feet and acanthus leaf decoration in carved and gilt wood.

89. **Table with Seasons, Flowers, and Fruit**
Rome, third quarter 19th century
Mosaic, marble, gilt wood
Diameter: 35½ in. (90.1 cm.)
Overall height: 37¼ in. (94.6 cm.)
Promised Gift (G 236)

Collection: Jossi Benjaminoff, New York.

130

This table top demonstrates the technical virtuosity of the Roman mosaicists of the nineteenth century. It includes five round paintings that create illusions of nature, each surrounded by an elaborate metal frame simulated in mosaic; the four outer pictures are separated by metal urns holding the fruits and flowers of the seasons, their various textures captured in mosaic.

The mosaics are set into black Belgian marble, which enhances the effect of relief. The center panel, bordered in lapis lazuli, shows a peasant family with their animals before a hut. The model, still in the Vatican Workshop, is unsigned but can be attributed to the Lombard painter Francesco Londonio (1723–1783); the same cartoon was used for cat. no. 90. The outer roundels represent the four seasons; their design source is not known but stylistic evidence indicates an artist active in Rome in the third quarter of the nineteenth century. Like the mosaic, the gilt and carved wood pedestal support is Italian from the third quarter of the nineteenth century.

This table top is similar in plan to one in the Hermitage,[1] but with obvious differences. In the Hermitage table, Rubens' *Romulus and Remus with the She-Wolf,* rather than the bucolic scene, is in the center; the four seasons are oval and smaller, the bouquets of flowers larger; pictures and urns are connected by festoons of flowers. The result is an overall tapestrylike pattern rather than the precise modeling and sharp contrast of flowers against the receding black marble background of the Gilbert table top.

1. Efimova, *Mozaika,* pp. 12, 110, pl. 75.

90. **Pastoral Scene**
Rome, late 19th century
Mosaic, black marble
11⅞ x 11⅞ in. (30.2 x 30.2 cm.)
m.77.1.25 (G 45)

Collection: J. Stolper, New York.

Exhibition: LACMA, no. 27; V & A, no. 17.

Literature: Sherman, *Gilbert,* pp. 16–17, repr. in color pl. II, with a detail.

This pastoral scene of a peasant family with their animals by a hut is based on an anonymous painting preserved in the Vatican Workshop. There is a drawing for the peasant woman with the basket of eggs by the Lombard artist Francesco Londonio (1723–1783) in the large group of drawings by him in the Ambrosiana, Milan. It can be assumed, therefore, that the prototype for this mosaic was either painted by Londonio or at least based on a composition by him. The subject must have been a popular one in the late nineteenth century. The same model was used for the center of a table top (cat. no. 89) and for another mosaic plaque in the Gilbert Collection (G 144).

91. Simonetti
Rome, active late 19th century
Satyr and Goat
Mosaic on slate
7½ x 10⅝ in. (19 x 27 cm.)
m.75.135.2 (G 2)

Collection: Chodes, New York.

Exhibitions: LACMA, no. 12; V & A, no. 3

Literature: Sherman, *Gilbert,* p. 27, repr. in color pl. IX.

On the back of this mosaic is a printed label "Rev. Fabbrica di S. Pietro in Vaticano—Studio del Musaico." In the space for identification of the object is the typewritten title "Fauno con capra;" in that for the name of the artist is written "Simonetti" in late nineteenth-century pen script. No further information about the artist has yet been found.

While the printed and written scripts on the label suggest that the mosaic was executed in the late nineteenth century, the cartoon derives from an ancient Roman composition that was also used to decorate porcelain.[1] It is possible that it was by Vincenzo Camuccini, who directed the Vatican Workshop until 1844, or by one of his assistants. A mosaic of an ancient sacrifice that was given by Gregory SVI to Czar Nicholas I in 1846 and that has some stylistic relationship to the Gilbert mosaic was based on a sketch by Camuccini.[2]

133

1. E. Romano, *Le porcellane di Capodimonte,* Naples, 1959, fig. 117.

2. Efimova, *Mozaika,* pp. 11, 101, pl. 61.

92. Decio Podio
Venice, born ca. 1860

Tigress

Mosaic

19 x 25 3/16 in. (48.3 x 64 cm.)

Signed, lower left: DECIO PODIO, VENEZIA

Promised Gift (G 150)

Collection: Blackwell Antique Gallery,
San Francisco.

Literature: Hillier, *Connoisseur,* p. 271, repr. fig. 5.

134

This rectangular mosaic showing a tiger in her lair is signed at lower left: "Decio Podio, Venezia." A member of a well-known family of artists and mosaicists, Decio Podio was born in Venice about 1860. His father, Enrico, was the head mosaicist of the Basilica of St. Mark's in Venice during the late nineteenth century. Members of the family still survive in Italy (Bologna and Rome) but they are unable to furnish further information about this artist.

The subject is taken either from a painting, *Tigress Lying below Rocks,* by George Stubbs (1724–1806) or from a 1798 mezzotint after it by John Murphy.[1] The mosaicist has transformed Stubb's heavy, lurking tigress into a sprightly cat.

1. W. S. Sparrow, *George Stubbs and Ben Marshall,* New York: Scribner's, 1929, pl. preceding p. 21.

93. **Table with Bird and Floral Design**
Florence, third quarter 19th century
Pietre dure, ebonized wood, gilt bronze
Height: 28 in. (71 cm.)
Width: 45½ in. (115.5 cm.)
Height of table: 28 in. (71 cm.)
m.77.1.90 (G 207)

Collection: Firestone and Parson, Boston.

The pietre dure panels, which include the top in flat mosaic and six side panels in bas-relief, are typical products of Florence in the third quarter of the nineteenth century. They were, however, not made in the Opificio but in one of the private workshops in Florence.

The table support is a perfect expression of French taste during the same period. Its design is vaguely inspired by Louis XVI prototypes, particularly the furniture of the cabinetmaker A. Weisweiler. There were a vast number of furniture makers working in Paris in the late nineteenth century, and little is known about their individual styles and methods. In the absence of a maker's stamp, it is virtually impossible to attribute this table to one of them.

135

Guéridon Top with Flowers
Florence, third quarter 19th century
Pietre dure, black marble, malachite
Diameter: 29⅛ in. (74 cm.)
Height of table: 28⅛ in. (71.4 cm.)
m.75.135.22 (G 65)

Collection: Anonymous, Los Angeles

Exhibition: LACMA, no. 42; V & A, no. 35.

This table top of black Belgian marble has a central bouquet of flowers in pietre dure with a malachite ribbon; on the outer edge are four swags of flowers.

A fine example of Florentine workmanship during the age of the International Exhibitions, this guéridon, or small round table, can be dated to the third quarter of the nineteenth century. While the quality is worthy of the Opificio, the substantial use of malachite makes it improbable that it was made there. A number of comparable round tables were made in the Opificio at the same period and some years earlier. The maker of the Gilbert guéridon must have known the table designed by G. B. Giorgi with a decoration of white roses,[1] the more elaborate one made by Nicolò Betti, or the one, still unattributed, with a wreath of magnolias.[2] Dr. Pampaloni Martelli has pointed out that there is a table top in the Musée Massena in Nice similar to the Gilbert top. The base, probably French, is in the form of a tripod with lyre ornamentation.

1. Rossi, *Mosaics,* pl. 92 in color.
2. Pampaloni Martelli, *Opificio,* pls. 56, 59.

95. Table with Still Life

Florence, late 19th century
Pietre dure
Height: 20 in. (50.8 cm.)
Width: 31⅜ in. (79.8 cm.)
Height of table: 31 in. (78.8 cm.)
m.77.1.96 (G 232)

Collection: Gwynby Antiques, Cleveland.

This type of illusionistic still life was introduced into the Florentine repertory in the eighteenth century and became especially popular in the last half of the nineteenth century. The surrealistic, meticulous treatment of the broken ledge on which the objects are displayed was first used in the Opificio by Antonio Cioci, who was active in Florence from 1722 to 1792, and later by his son, Leopoldo.[1] The Gilbert table, however, seems to have been made not in the Opificio but in a private workshop in Florence. This is confirmed by the presence of malachite in the ribbon, a stone never used in the Opificio.

The objects on the table are clues to dating the mosaic. They include a "Greek" vase and a "Roman" bronze lamp, a "Renaissance" ewer and some modern utensils. They represent a mélange of styles typical of the end of the nineteenth century.

The base of the table, which can be adjusted to show the top like a picture on an easel, is also an expression of Italian decorative art of the same period.

138

1. Rossi, *Mosaics,* pl. 91 in color.

96. Tarantoni
Rome, active late 19th–early 20th century
Cavalier
Mosaic
18¹¹/₁₆ x 10⅝ in. (47.4 x 27.1 cm.)
Signed, lower right: Tarantoni, R.F.S.P.V.
Promised Gift (G 70)

Collection: Herbert Trigger, New York.

Exhibitions: LACMA, no. 23; V & A, no. 4.

This rectangular mosaic showing a cavalier in seventeenth-century costume leaning on a sword is signed at the lower right "Tarantoni R. F. S. P. V." The abbreviation stands for "Reverenda Fabbrica di S. Pietro in Vaticano," the institution under whose jurisdiction the mosaic workshop operated. Tarantoni's name does not appear among the employees of the Vatican Mosaic Workshop but he must have been active there at the end of the nineteenth century or in the early decades of the twentieth.

97. Tarantoni
Rome, active late 19th–early 20th century
Musketeer
Mosaic
20⅞ x 12⅜ in. (53 x 31.5 cm.)
Signed, lower right: R. F. S. Petri Tarantoni
m.77.1.14 (G 10)

Collection: Steven Lewis, London.

Literature: Sherman, *Gilbert,* p. 38, repr. in color
pl. XVII.

140

The soldier in this rectangular mosaic wears a seventeenth-century costume and carries a musket, sword, and powder flask. On the lower right is the signature of the mosaicist, Tarantoni, under the letters "R. F. S. Petri," an abbreviation for "Reverenda Fabbrica Sancti Petri." The only other work of Tarantoni known to the author is the *Cavalier* in the Gilbert Collection (cat. no. 96).

98. **Drinking Cavalier**
Rome, late 19th–early 20th century
Mosaic
5½ x 4¹/₃₂ in. (14 x 10.4 cm.)
Promised Gift (G 41)

Exhibitions: LACMA, no. 24; V & A, no. 14.

Literature: Sherman, *Gilbert,* p. 39, repr. in color
pl. XVIII.

The mosaic is unsigned, but a comparison with cat. nos. 96 and 97 by Tarantoni suggests that like them it was probably made in Rome at the end of the nineteenth century or the beginning of the twentieth century. The somewhat more painterly treatment of the subject may, in fact, suggest the later date.

99. Mario Montelatici
Florence, 1894–1974
Two Little Tykes
Pietre dure
18⅞ x 13¾ in. (48 x 35 cm.)
Signed, lower left: Montelatici
Promised Gift (G 59)

Mario Montelatici was one of the last craftsmen in the Florentine tradition of great personal ability and virtuosity. He was born in Florence in 1894 to a family of mosaicists. In 1912 his father, Giovanni, was a founder of the "Arte del Mosaico," a private workshop still active in Florence on Via S. Giuseppe, just off the Piazza Sta. Croce. The shop was especially active in the first quarter of this century filling commissions for the king of Siam. Giovanni trained his son Mario and Fernando Ghisio, both of whom are represented in the Gilbert Collection. Mario worked in Florence throughout his life and died there in 1974.[1]

In this picture in pietre dure, Mario Montelatici has selected and joined his stones in a manner that suggests a continuously varied play of light through the picture, a style influenced by the Macchiaioli and the Impressionists of the past century. The prototype, however, is not a work of one of these masters but a cartoon of a type, charming and a little sentimental, used to illustrate popular periodicals in the early decades of this century.

142

1. Information kindly furnished by Mitello Montelatici, son of Mario; F. Ghisio; and B. Lastrucci, one of the present owners of the Arte del Mosaico.

100. Fernando Ghisio
Florence, born 1908
The Catch
Pietre dure
28⅛ x 18⅞ in. (75.5 x 48 cm.)
Signed, lower left: Fernando Ghisio
Promised Gift (G 37)

In this pietre dure picture of two boys in a hilly landscape, the older boy shows the younger one a glass jar with a frog he caught in the stream that flows beneath the bridge. The mosaicist who signed the work, Fernando Ghisio, was a pupil of Giovanni Montelatici and a colleague of his son, Mario; he resides in Florence in the Via del Campuccio.

Ghisio's style is considerably different from Mario's as exemplified by cat. no. 99. He is not concerned, as Montelatici was, with a brilliant pervading light, but is instead preoccupied with the tangible reality of the stone and the convincing three-dimensionality of his forms. It is a style that could readily be adapted to translating into pietre dure the paintings of contemporary Italian realists like Renato Guttuso.

This catalog was designed
in Los Angeles by Greg Thomas.

The text was set by R S Typographics.
Color preparation and lithography on
Consolidated's Productolith were by
Graphic Press.